THE GOON SHOW
COMPANION

THE
GOON SHOW
COMPANION

A History and Goonography

Written and compiled by
ROGER WILMUT

With a personal memoir by
JIMMY GRAFTON

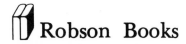 Robson Books

FIRST PUBLISHED IN GREAT BRITAIN IN 1976 BY ROBSON
BOOKS LTD., 28 POLAND STREET, LONDON W1V 3DB.
COPYRIGHT © 1976 ROGER WILMUT & JIMMY GRAFTON.
SCRIPT EXTRACTS COPYRIGHT ©1976 SPIKE MILLIGAN, ERIC
SYKES, THE ESTATE OF LARRY STEPHENS.

ISBN 0 903895 64 1

First impression May 1976
Second impression October 1976
Third impression September 1981

The authors would like to thank Spike Milligan, Eric Sykes and Mrs
Diana Hewitt for permission to quote from the scripts. Thanks are also
due to Mrs Hewitt for permission to reproduce Larry Stephens's
drawings, both in the book and on the cover.

Printed in Hungary

CONTENTS

FOURWORD

BY THE GOONS

It is hard to believe that somebody has actually written a TEXTBOOK on the Goon Shows. I can only wonder at the endurance of Roger Wilmut, who has got so much technological evidence together, because I know how difficult it is to get anything from the BBC which is more than a year old. It took me more than two years' writing to them to get a complete list of the Goon Shows they were holding. So if nothing else this little volume has taken a great amount of midnight oil (£1.30 a gallon, available at good grocers).

I wish the book well, but I cannot help feeling that it's my obituary.

Spike Milligan

Thousands of words have been written about 'The Goon Show' and its participants — not all of them true. If anyone can produce a definitive biography, Jimmy Grafton is the man. His pub at Westminster was our first meeting place, and when 'The Goon Show' was born he provided the hot water, the forceps and the brandy for the patient. We had to be patient — the service was terrible. He has been my agent for twenty-five years. He is still my friend.

Harry Secombe

6

My name is Peter Sellers. I am a human being. Several years ago I took part in the BBC Radio Goon Shows. I was called upon to produce humorous sounds and voices, which I did to the best of my ability. Two gentlemen appearing in the same show were named S. Milligan and H. Secombe. Also, there was a Peruvian Intelligence Officer, Michael Bentine.

I was paid certain monies for my appearances. They were very small.

When I first visited Major Grafton's public house in Victoria I was five years old. I am now ninety-two, and still enjoy a good laugh.

Peter Sellers

To the numerous people who have interviewed me about the deep sociological meaning of 'The Goon Show', I always give the same answer. We had a ball doing it and I only left it reluctantly because of pressing business. I look back on it all with a great deal of affection and pleasure. If there was any hidden factor not known to the audience, it was that we were all smashed out of our heads with the sheer joy of living.

Michael Bentine

PREFACE

'The Goon Show' can be seen, in retrospect, to have played a highly significant rôle in the history of British comedy, quite apart from becoming something of a 'cult' in its own right. In view of this, it seems only fitting to chronicle both its beginning and its subsequent development in enough detail to satisfy the serious student of such matters, as well as the army of fans around the world who have given it their enthusiastic support and interest.

Some of the actual Goon Show scripts have been published, accompanied by much amusing Milligana; and in addition, the private lives of the individual Goons have been and continue to be dealt with in a variety of biographical literature. The present volume, however, has a more closely defined purpose — to set down what is, in effect, a biography of 'The Goon Show' itself.

Roger Wilmut, with the assistance of Tim Smith and Peter Copeland, has traced the history and development of the programmes, the characters, and Milligan's individual humour; and has compiled a detailed 'Goonography' which gives a full listing of the shows themselves, together with other relevant information.

Jimmy Grafton, friend and confidant of the Goons, has contributed his own personal story of the formative years (with perhaps some inadvertent disregard for chronology), endeavouring to include only such reminiscences and individual history as may throw some light on the personalities and characters of the Goons themselves. Some biographical information has been drawn from an earlier (unpublished) work by D. J. Hall of Worthing.

R.F.W.

J.D.G.

I

A HISTORY

of

'THE

GOON SHOW'

BEFORE THE GOONS

At first sight it seems odd that the BBC, whose public image in the 1950s was that of a starchy maiden aunt, could have adopted such an unlikely set of nephews as the Goons. However, Auntie, though a little strait-laced, had never lacked a sense of humour — even in the 1930s, when the BBC radiated an aura of unbending respectability. Though the image which remains today is that of announcers reading the news in dinner-jackets, and programmes of a distinctly edifying nature, there was still a spirit of adventure about radio, and developments and changes were taking place all the time.

Until the late 1930s the BBC's comedy output was drawn entirely from the outside world of music hall and Variety. Well-known comedians like Harry Tate, Billy Bennett, Will Hay and Max Miller did versions of their acts suitably modified for radio. A few artists retained a standard format — for instance, Mabel Constanduros with 'The Bugginses', and Harry Hemsley with his imaginary family of small children — but there were no comedy series as we know them today. The artists appeared in programmes constructed on the lines of a music hall bill, with a different set of acts each week. It is surprising that it took so long for the idea of series comedy to arrive. When 'Band Waggon' was first broadcast on January 5, 1938 it was a completely new departure: Arthur Askey and Richard Murdoch starred in a regular series of hour-long programmes. The real breakthrough was in the running theme of Askey and Murdoch living in a flat in Broadcasting House. A large section of the public took this quite seriously, and the fan mail to this mythical address was enormous.

The show was so successful that the Variety Department was soon looking around for another comedy series. Their idea was to imitate the 'George Burns and Gracie Allen Show' in the USA; the man they picked to build the show round was Tommy Handley. Mercifully, the idea of imitating Burns and Allen disappeared fairly early on in the

13

proceedings. Ted Kavanagh was asked to write the scripts (the title was 'It's That Man Again'), and on July 12, 1939 the first 'ITMA' programme went on the air. The format was a highly successful one, with each show having a vague plot, interrupted by two musical items. Handley remained 'on-stage' as the central character around whom all the chaos revolved; the other characters came on in ones and twos. Mrs Mopp, Colonel Chinstrap, Mr What's-'is-name, Ali Oop, Claude and Cecil, Lefty, the Diver — all these characters entered the listeners' imaginations, and people quoted the show's catchphrases at each other in the most unlikely situations.

By the middle of the 4th series the show had reached a very high standard of production, which it managed to maintain right through to the end in 1949. If the show did not develop any further after the 4th series, at least it did not deteriorate. It was this 'plateau' that the Goons were later to reach before building their extraordinary, rather unstable but brilliant edifice of humour.

The success of 'ITMA' led to a number of radio series — 'Much-Binding-in-the-Marsh' was one particularly good example. The standard variety format was established fairly rapidly — two musical items separating three sketches, either individual or linked to form a vague plot. By 1948 the idea of the radio comedy series was only ten years old, but already attempts were being made to break away from the established patterns. A series called 'Listen, My Children' ran for eight shows between June 1 and July 20, 1948 in the Home Service. The producer was Pat Dixon (who later encouraged and eventually produced the Goons), and the artists were Robert Beatty, Jon Pertwee, Peter Watson, Carole Carr, Benny Lee, Benny Hill, Patricia Hayes, and an up-and-coming young comic called Harry Secombe. The show deliberately set out to avoid the established traditions of radio comedy — there were no regular characters, no catchphrases, and no studio audiences. The sketches were witty, often with a satirical edge; the style was vaguely similar to a later Pat Dixon production, 'Bedtime with Braden', and also foreshadowed some aspects of the early Goon Show scripts.

A follow-up series to 'Listen, My Children' was planned, originally under the title 'Falling Leaves'; however it was decided that the series should be placed on the Third Programme, in the hope of appealing to an educated minority audience. The title was changed to 'Third Division — Some Vulgar Fractions', these being Robert Beatty, Benny Lee, Bruce Belfrage, Patricia Hayes, Harry Secombe, Benny Hill, Carole Carr, Margaret Lindsay, Robert Moreton, and two more up-and-coming comics called Peter Sellers and Michael Bentine. There were six shows, running weekly from 26-1-49 (see Appendix 4). The producer was again Pat Dixon, and the scripts were written by

14

Frank Muir and Denis Norden, with additional material by Paul Dehn. The second programme had a sketch for Peter Sellers which is familiar today — 'Balham, Gateway to the South', later performed again by Sellers for issue on a long-playing record.

'Band Waggon', 'ITMA', 'Listen, My Children', 'Third Division'; one could mention others — 'Danger, Men At Work', which also dispensed with an audience, Muir and Norden's 'Take It From Here' — all helped to expand the vocabulary of radio comedy and take it further away from its music-hall origins.

It was into this situation that the Goons came — four bright young comedians, one of them a brilliant scriptwriter in the making — all with the idea of turning BBC radio comedy on its head. The blending of these four elements began in the ancient Westminster hostelry known as 'Grafton's'. Its then host, ex-infantry-officer turned publican, City Councillor and scriptwriter, Jimmy Grafton — in whose family the pub had been since 1848 — was the primary catalyst in this gradual but significant chemical reaction. Christened 'KOGVOS' or 'Keeper of Goons and Voice of Sanity', he tells his own story of the coalescence of these ingredients into 'The Goon Show'.

THE BIRTH OF THE GOONS

A Personal Memoir by Jimmy Grafton

In 1946, newly demobilised from the army, with a wife and two small children to support, I had launched myself on the dual careers of pub licensee and radio script-writer; the first to keep a roof over our heads, the second to fulfil an urge that had already impelled me to write shows for the entertainment of my unit while awaiting demob. By 1948 I was contributing regularly to radio Variety in programmes such as 'The Forces Show', 'Workers' Playtime', 'Variety Bandbox', and numerous others that offered chances for stardom — or at least recognition — to the post-war crop of comedians, most of them ex-servicemen. These radio shows were the breeding ground that produced such enduring stars as Tony Hancock, Petula Clark, Terry-Thomas, Max Bygraves, Beryl Reid, Dick Emery, Julie Andrews, Frankie Howerd, Alfred Marks, Joan Turner, Janet Brown, Joan Sims, Bob Monkhouse, and many others. They also provided valuable initial experience for later top-ranking script-writers like Muir and Norden, Galton and Simpson, Eric Sykes, Sid Colin, Talbot Rothwell and Larry Stephens. Three of the Goons also had their early individual and separate exposure doing solo 'turns' on such programmes: Michael Bentine, in partnership with Tony Sherwood, had a wild but original act called, typically, 'Sherwood and Forrest'; Peter Sellers did brilliant impressions; Harry Secombe, not yet singing 'straight', clowned verbally and vocally.

The most notable of these programmes was perhaps 'Variety Bandbox', which ran continuously for some years under the guidance of Joy Russell-Smith, and was responsible more than any other radio show of the time for introducing new talent to a radio audience. It was not only wide-ranging in its use of individual vocal and comedy talents, but also provided budding script-writers with the opportunity of writing sketch material, and even introduced on the air, in the rôle of 'commères', such rising young Rank film starlets or charm school protégées as Margaret Lockwood, Valerie Hobson, Jean Kent, Ann Todd, Patricia Roc and Googie Withers.

An important point about the show was that it had a 'resident comedian', which meant that the artiste lucky enough to be chosen would have the chance to be heard regularly over a period of time — an invaluable contribution to any youngster's career. I had begun writing scripts for ex-Geraldo band singer-turned-comedian, Derek Roy, and naturally I was overjoyed to learn that he was to be appointed the first resident comedian. This meant regular fortnightly appearances — which meant regular fortnightly payments as far as I was concerned.

My joy was not unalloyed, however. One lunchtime, two odd-looking characters, both shock-headed and bespectacled, walked into my pub and ordered drinks. One of them was Michael Bentine, to whom I had already been introduced by a mutual friend. The other was someone he wanted me to meet, whom he regarded as another rising young comedy star. This comparatively slim gentleman with the cherubic countenance, humorous mouth and eyes and high-pitched giggle, turned out to be Harry Secombe. After the introductions, the conversation turned to radio and radio comedy. It transpired that both Harry and Mike were somewhat critical of 'Variety Bandbox' and its resident comedian, considering his material to be rather corny. As good-humouredly as I could, I admitted to being the author. It might have been an embarrassing moment, but instead we had a good laugh and some convivial drinking, following which the pair announced that they would be back the next day. It must have come as some surprise to them when, returning the following lunchtime, they commenced a conversation with mine host, who gazed at them in amazement and with a total lack of recognition. They had unknowingly approached my twin brother Peter, who was a regular luncher in the pub. Once again we had something to laugh about.

This readiness to laugh and derive as much enjoyment as possible out of almost any situation was a common bond which embraced also Spike and Peter, both of whom I was shortly to meet. The pub became a sort of 'home-from-home' for all of them, and in the course of time I got to know much more about my new friends.

Michael Bentine was the first of the ultimate Goon quartet that I met. Member of a well (and widely) connected Peruvian family, the Bentins, Mike was born in Watford on 26 January, 1922, and brought up in England. He finished his education at Eton, and subsequently joined the R.A.F., performing his war service in a variety of jobs. Some of these he would talk about; others he would refer to only with hints of mysterious adventures in strange places. Knowing Mike as we came to, we took a few of his stories with a pinch of salt. His undoubted intelligence and abilities were accompanied by a powerful, creative imagination which was forever fantasising interesting experiences into fascinating exploits.

I have heard him give accounts of exciting incidents as a fighter pilot, bomber pilot, parachutist, commando, member of the Secret Service, even as an atomic scientist. His claims to be an expert swordsman, pistol shot and archer are substantially true, as I have verified with my own eyes. He is also a qualified glider pilot. But one of his greatest talents was for the spontaneous invention of intriguing stories about himself, rather in the manner of a modern Baron Münchausen. These tales he would sprinkle with erudite literary and scientific allusions or recondite facts of some kind or another. I was prone at first to quote Alexander Pope at him: 'The bookful blockhead, ignorantly read,/With loads of learned lumber in his head', but because of the extent of his real knowledge, I came to realise this was a calumny, and to regard him more in terms of Goldsmith's village schoolmaster: 'words of learned length, and thundering sound,/Amazed the gazing rustics ranged around;/And still they gazed and still their wonder grew/That one small head could carry all he knew'.

Let me give an example. One evening a year or two after we had met, when Mike was well-established as an entertainer, I visited him at the old London Hippodrome on the corner of Coventry Street (now the Talk of the Town), where he was appearing in a revue. I had actually gone there to discuss the collections of weapons we had each 'liberated' during the war — all, I hasten to add, subsequently handed in to the authorities. Mike had borrowed a German hunting rifle I had acquired and had promised to find a telescopic sight for it. I never did discover what became of that rifle, but it somehow went astray and in return Mike presented me later with a small, nickel-plated ladies' Colt revolver (with an interesting history, it goes without saying).

On the night in question he was in his dressing-room, experimenting with a *long-bow*. To demonstrate the penetrative power of the arrows, he fired one at the dressing-room door. The penetration was aptly proved, since it went through the door and projected two or three inches out the other side, much to the consternation of an approaching visitor, who turned out to be a young reporter from the now defunct newspaper, the *News Chronicle*. This eager young man had come to interview Michael, and this he proceeded to do in my presence.

After getting the usual background information and details of the show in which Michael was appearing, he then asked the sort of challenging question that was always the blue touchpaper of Mike's rocketing imagination: 'Are you working on anything else at the moment?' Mike's eyes lit up and so did the touchpaper. 'Yes, indeed,' said he. 'Actually, I'm working on my new film.' 'That sounds interesting,' said the reporter. 'What's it all about?' 'Science fiction,' replied Mike promptly. 'It's about an invasion of the earth from another planet.' By now the reporter was busily scribbling in his notepad. Mike then went on to describe the idea of the film, how gigantic creatures from outer space would descend on an English town, crawling over the rooftops and so on.

I must say I was as fascinated as the reporter and just as eager for Mike to answer his next question, which was how such an incident could be represented in the film. The answer posed no difficulty for Mike. 'Well, obviously,' he said, 'we shall be using model sets and the creatures will be represented by ants. African driver ants, actually.' I had never heard of these, but I had no doubt that they existed. Mike then added as an afterthought, 'Of course, as the film is in colour, we shall have them dyed red with cochineal.' There was, of course, not a word of truth in the whole story. Mike was as usual exercising his imagination and amusing himself and me at the reporter's expense. This, however, did not prevent a quite sizable item appearing in the paper the following day describing Michael Bentine's interesting new film.

There was one occasion when I thought I might have caught Michael out in one of these self-indulgent little fantasies, but it was not to be. It happened early one morning at a Goon Show rehearsal, when I encountered him in the studio at Aeolian Hall in Bond Street, busy preparing some mechanical prop—another activity in which he has always excelled. It was the morning that most newspapers had carried the story of the defection to the Russians of Bruno Pontecorvo, an Italian-born atomic scientist working in Britain. The news seemed to make Michael very sad. 'Poor Pontecorvo,' he said. 'What a terrible thing. You know, he and I worked side by side doing atomic research.' I raised my eyebrows. 'Are you sure it was the same fellow?' 'Yes, of course, I knew him well. Poor old Guiseppe.' At once I thought I had him. 'Just a moment, Mike,' I said, 'Pontecorvo's name is Bruno.' Mike didn't turn a hair. 'I know that,' he said, 'but we always used to call him Guiseppe.'

We've had many laughs at Mike's expense over the years about his tall stories, but he's had just as many laughs on us when some of the tallest have turned out to be true.

In a practical sense, his great ingenuity and imagination were not only carried into script writing for himself and others, with considerable success, but also into his cabaret performances. His act, in which he used the broken back of a chair in an incredible variety of ways to illustrate a stirring call to Britain to unite, was a classic. I called at his house in Chelsea once, to find him in the throes of trying out a most ingenious portable set for a quick-change artiste, which he had not only invented, but also built. Successive generations of children have been enthralled by his Bumblies and Pottys and other delightful creations.

Over the years Mike has maintained an unconquerable enthusiasm and enjoyment of life, despite personal tragedies. I have always found him gentlemanly, kind and considerate, and his decision to leave 'The Goon Show' at an early stage in its development (more of this later) in no way reduced the friendship we all still enjoy.

My closest friend from the Goon Show days is, of course, Harry Secombe, whom I subsequently managed and represented. Harry's talents have developed in a variety of directions: comedian, singer, actor, writer, artist, photographer — as all of these he has proved his excellence. In those early days his generous good nature and sense of fun were much in evidence, but his natural humility made each new step along the way of his career a tentative one, accompanied by agonies of self-doubt.

When I first met him he was already launched on the sea of comedy, in radio and in vaudeville. He had begun his career, in fact, in the army, having left his Swansea home and his job as a tea-boy in a steel-works to volunteer for military service. He had seen action in North Africa as a lance bombardier with the Royal Artillery, and finally had been seconded to Combined Services Entertainment in what was known as the Central Pool of Artists — a move which his obvious and natural flair for comic self-expression made almost inevitable.

There are many humorous incidents in Harry's army life which appear in other biographical accounts, and about which he himself has written. It is, however, perhaps relevant at this point to mention one or two of these. Harry has always possessed the comedic advantage of a countenance which can, at will, assume an aspect of beaming idiocy. This effect can be heightened by wearing headgear low enough over the forehead to give his face a look of near-lunacy.

One day in the desert, Field Marshal Montgomery was haranguing a gathering of troops. It was the usual Monty pep talk along the lines of 'You men are doing a great job', etc. etc. Immediately below the back of the staff car from which he was speaking sat a group of soldiers, amongst whom was Lance Bombardier Secombe. In ill-fitting battledress, beret down to his eyebrows, and burdened with a pair of metal-rim spectacles previously broken and now held together by insulating tape, which cocked them at an angle across his nose, Harry must have looked a very strange manifestation of the British military presence in North Africa.

During his peroration, Monty allowed his glance to drop downwards, meeting the earnest gaze of the Lance Bombardier's upturned face. Momentarily unnerved by the apparition, Monty paused. Feeling obliged to say something, Harry nodded his head encouragingly. 'We're with you, Mr Montgomery,' he said. 'Yes,' muttered Monty uncertainly, and continued, but without allowing himself any further glances in Harry's direction.

Making people laugh has been habitual with Harry from quite an early age, and it is a rôle in life he has always enjoyed. It had its drawbacks in the army, however, such as the occasion when he decided to apply to his Commanding Officer to be considered for a commission. Having been marched into his C.O.'s presence, he explained his request while the C.O. gazed thoughtfully at him. 'You want to become an officer, Secombe?' 'Yes, sir.' 'And you're serious?' 'Yes, sir.' The C.O. began to smile; the smile became a chuckle; the chuckle became a laugh; by which time both Harry and the accompanying Warrant Officer had joined in. After a few moments of enjoyable hysteria, Lance Bombardier Secombe was marched out again

Having been seconded to C.P.A., Harry was one day mounting the stairs to the office of the colonel in charge of entertainment. As he did so, the colonel started to descend. Noticing a rather unmilitary scarf that Harry was wearing with his battledress, he barked at him, 'Take that bloody scarf off!' — virtually the only words he spoke to Harry until after the war. The colonel was Philip Slessor, who later became a BBC announcer, and the next time he met Harry was on 'Variety Bandbox'. After their previous one and only encounter, Harry was amused to hear Philip introduce him as 'My old wartime comrade'!

Like so many of us, Harry thoroughly enjoyed the fun and comradeship of the army, despite some of the disadvantages, and since the war he has devoted a great deal of time to freely entertaining the Forces all over the world. For his services to the Army Benevolent Fund, he was awarded the C.B.E.

Demobbed in 1946 and determined to make his career in show business, Harry, when we met, had already made his professional début at London's Windmill Theatre and was sampling the delights—or otherwise—of touring in Variety shows. One revue, 'Forces Showboat', featured a chorus of male drag artistes, including the one destined to become the greatest of them all, Danny La Rue.

Danny, a generous person himself, recalls most of all Harry's genuine good nature and kindness. On one occasion at Wolverhampton, Danny fell and broke his forearm. Harry drove him to the hospital between performances and had him back at the theatre in time for the second house, with his arm in plaster and camouflaged with a fur muff. That Christmas, when heavy snow had curtailed the business so much that the theatre, with the banks closed, could only pay the artistes minimally in cash, Harry provided the cast with money from his own pocket so that they could pay their fares home and have something over for Christmas—a gesture that Danny has never forgotten.

Harry's music hall act, which he had originated in the army, consisted mainly of two items: first, a hilarious demonstration, practically in mime, of the different ways in which men shave, involving the use of shaving soap and water and a blunt cut-throat razor. The whole act was quite zany and finished with Harry drinking the shaving water. He resurrected it recently during a television interview and it was just as funny as ever.

This routine did once result, however, in Harry's being paid off (for the only time in his career) at a theatre in Bolton, Lancashire, where, after the opening performance, the manager sent for him, told him 'You'll not bloody shave in my time', and sent him packing. Despite his disappointment, the irrepressible Harry sent a telegram to Michael Bentine: 'Audience with me all the way. Managed to shake them off at the station.'

The second part of his act was an impression of the duet 'Sweethearts', made famous by film musical stars Jeanette MacDonald and Nelson Eddy. Harry sang both the tenor and soprano with an altercation in the middle that went:

TENOR   When we were sweethearts in June —
SOPRANO   May.
TENOR   June.
SOPRANO   May.
TENOR   June.
SOPRANO   May.
TENOR   Oh — (*raspberry*).

That raspberry of Harry's became famous. He used it during the verbal part of his act to anticipate the reaction of his audience to certain deliberately corny jokes, blowing the raspberry and saying quickly, 'I was first!' Interestingly, he was, at the same time, unconsciously betraying the diffidence and humility that underlies his whole character.

As a child in Swansea (where he was born on 8 September, 1921), his eyesight had deteriorated after an attack of measles; in the theatre he was to discover that by removing his spectacles he could reduce the audience to a reassuring blur — with not a hostile gaze in sight. The same shyness had made him unable as a boy to sing for his parents and relatives without first closeting himself in the outside loo — if the family was still sitting inside the house, it might well explain how he developed his vocal projection! It certainly took a lot of encouragement and a degree of nagging to persuade him even to contemplate singing seriously at the start of his professional career.

The first public occasion was in a radio series early in 1950, called 'Welsh Rarebit', produced by the formidable Mai Jones, composer of the song that has virtually become a second Welsh national anthem: 'We'll Keep A Welcome'. With much trepidation, Harry had agreed to finish his comedy spot with a song, seriously sung. Also, I urged, it should have a 'straight' introduction that would indicate to the audience that this was in no way an extension of the preceding comedy. Harry accordingly delivered this in an appropriately grave manner; the musical introduction commenced, then suddenly over the top of it came Harry's voice, loud and clear: 'Stand by for blasting!'

Nevertheless, the song went down extremely well, though a different reaction awaited a later vocal offering, this time on 'Variety Bandbox'. Harry was to close his act with 'Only Make-Believe' from the musical *Showboat*, accompanied by Billy Ternent and his orchestra, and in front of a large theatre audience. For the musically-minded, let me explain that the last line of this vocally rather wide-ranging song is 'For to tell the truth, I do', and the straightforward way to sing it is for the penultimate note of 'I' to be sung a tone above the last note on the word 'do'; in this case, musically speaking, from top G to top F. Since the interval from 'truth' to 'I' is a jump of an octave and a third, it was difficult enough for Harry to pitch it in any event; unfortunately, before the broadcast he was subjected to a barrage of suggested 'better' finishes. These varied from singing A instead of G on the word 'I', followed by the flourish of a three-part 'do-o-o' on A, G and F, to the ambitious proposal of an ex-tenor friend (in this case, almost a tenor ex-friend), the late Percy Manchester, who urged that Harry should on the word 'I' slide up from the A to a top C, before hitting the triple noted 'do'.

If *you're* confused, imagine Harry's state of mind. His anxiety was contagious and seemed to communicate itself to the audience as we all waited with bated breath for the climax. He sang well, with the usual *rallentando* on 'To tell the truth', with a *tacet* from the orchestra. In the split second that followed, the atmosphere was electric. Then Harry hit a high note that managed to be in between everything that had ever been suggested. Desperately trying to recover, his voice slid quickly around this musical no-man's land, becoming a manic shriek as, throwing his arms in the air, he retreated to his last line of comic defence and fell flat on his back. For a brief moment there was an awestruck silence, then the whole place erupted. I have never in my life seen an audience more hysterical with mirth. Even Billy Ternent dropped his baton and was doubled up with laughter. Then the mirth turned to applause and the applause to cheers. A near-disaster had become something of a triumph.

Like disaster and triumph, tragedy and comedy are so finely divided that almost any situation, heading for but narrowly missing the former and incidentally producing the latter, will generate an explosion of mirth; and the more sudden the anticlimax the greater the explosion. Identification makes us laugh at the predicaments of others, providing their suffering is ultimately unharmful.

Harry was involved in another scene of audience hysteria when singing soprano to Terry-Thomas's baritone in a hilarious version of the 'Miserere' duet from *Il Trovatore*, basically a comedy situation, the strength of which was that a serious attempt was being made to sing it well. Terry-Thomas recalls having to make Harry face away from him in order to be able to continue without breaking up. The tension built with their success, and was dissolved into laughter by their ultimate failure—a gradual crumbling of their efforts into a final glorious shambles that had the audience rocking. In certain hands, it seems, music not only 'hath charms to soothe a savage breast' but also to make it heave with mirth! Terry once jokingly suggested that the only reason the two of them did not become a double act was that their combined initials—TTHS—were also those of his real name, Thomas Terry Hoare-Stevens, which would have been unfair to Harry.

However, these events were still in the future. Meanwhile, I had yet to meet the eventual Goon of Goons. When not on tour, Harry had been living at 13 Linden Gardens with ex-service friends Johnny Mulgrew and Spike Milligan, two-thirds of a comedy and musical act known as the Bill Hall Trio. Another occupant of the room was comedy star-to-be, Norman Vaughan. There were others who came and went, but since the room was basically let to two, a certain amount of subterfuge was necessary to keep the truth from the landlady. On one occasion some of Spike's clothing had to be thrown from the window to avoid discovery, though to other tenants the occupation seemed peaceful and well-behaved. It had to be.

It was inevitable that, having met Harry, it would not be long before I encountered his close friend, Spike.

Spike Milligan

Spike was probably the most complex member of the quartet of Goons, but as the ultimate mainspring of 'The Goon Show', worthy of the closest study. All the Goons, like most compulsive comedians, were manic depressives to some degree. Spike's highs and lows were the most extreme, swinging from a state of euphoria in which he was happy, out-going and spontaneously funny, to the complete opposite, when he became brooding and uncommunicative, harbouring dark suspicions and a desire to hide from the world.

The child is father to the man, and a glimpse into Spike's early history may serve to reveal some of the influences that helped to shape his later attitudes.

The son of an army N.C.O. hailing from Southern Ireland, Spike was born in India on 16 April, 1918, and educated at Roman Catholic convent schools in Poona and Rangoon. The breaks in his schooling left him with a somewhat sketchy education. In addition, until his father, Leo Milligan, was promoted to Regimental Sergeant Major, the family's standard of living was not exactly high. For a year or two their lot improved, but in 1933 when Spike was fifteen, Ramsay MacDonald's government imposed a ten per cent cut on the armed forces which brought Leo Milligan, at the age of forty, back into Civvy Street with no job and a pension of fifty shillings a week. Spike resumed his schooling at St Saviour's in Lewisham, walking the three miles from their home in Catford to save the bus fare. Although the family fortunes later improved, this was a depressing time, especially for a young lad as sensitive as Spike. His early experiences of life bred in him a detestation of officialdom and the establishment in general, including the military.

Not drawn, as Harry was, towards literature as a recreational escape from the world, Spike took up the trumpet, at one time setting his sights on a musical career. Came the war, however, and Spike found himself a gunner in the Royal Artillery. His meeting with Harry has been described elsewhere, but bears repeating here. Briefly, this took place in North Africa, when Lance Bombardier Secombe's detachment was at the base of a small escarpment on top of which another unit were digging gun emplacements. One gun fired without being properly dug in, recoiling down the escarpment close to the Secombe tent. Harry's first view of Spike was an Eccles-like apparition voicing the query, 'Anybody seen a gun?'

Later, Spike, having been blown up at Monte Cassino — a nerve-shattering experience, which no doubt took its toll of his stability — found himself in the same convalescent hospital as Harry. Spike's obvious comedy persona earmarked him also as a potential performer for the amusement of the troops — which in any case he seems to have been doing most of the time! — and thus began an enduring friendship that took them together through many a hilarious experience in Combined Services Entertainment.

This was a particularly happy time for Spike. Playing his trumpet and making people laugh were the two things he most enjoyed. His natural indiscipline was also no doubt given more rein in the necessarily laxer atmosphere of military showbiz.

For a brief period at the end of the war, he continued as a member of the Bill Hall Trio, featuring music and comedy, until finally the trio broke up and Spike found himself looking for a career, and spending many hours at Allen's Club, near the Windmill Theatre, in the company of Mike Bentine, Frank Muir, Jimmy Edwards, and others.

Spike's creative impulse for comedy was now stirring in him thoughts of script-writing. His mind was full of ideas, some of them brilliantly inventive and comic, but his ability to express them on paper was limited. Harry decided that I, as an already practising script-writer with the added advantage of a pub, was the person Spike should meet. Thus it was that one evening I was introduced to a slim, good-looking young man, whose air of slight melancholy could suddenly erupt into manic glee, often ending in a tearful hysteria of laughter.

His early attempts at written work were an incredible mixture of funny lines and bad spelling, nonsensical padding and nonexistent punctuation; but through it all was discernible the unmistakable promise of a great comic talent. Untutored as Spike may have been then, it was evident that the more he learned of his craft, the better he would become.

As the coterie in Linden Gardens had broken up, Spike was looking for a temporary home. It would obviously be an advantage for him to stay at the pub, where we could work together more closely. With a wife and two children to accommodate, plus some staff, I had no room for him other than a large attic. However, with the aid of a mattress, some bedding and a chest of drawers, all was made ready and Spike moved in. The others immediately christened him 'The Prisoner of Zenda', but Spike had lived in far worse conditions in the army, without the ready access to food and drink now available to him. He was quite happy, and together we set to work.

Since I was writing for Derek Roy, who wanted to progress from 'Variety Bandbox' to a series, we conceived a programme rather cornily entitled 'Hip Hip Hoo Roy'. The series did not exactly break any windows, but we had great fun writing it and many a long night was punctuated by shrieks of laughter at jokes that amused us, if not the listeners.

The most interesting point about this series was that it used a story line as opposed to sketch comedy, a technique that Spike returned to in the later development of 'The Goon Show'. The show also introduced the character of Eccles, though not yet under that name. Eccles, I have always maintained, is the real Milligan; his id or alter ego; a simple, happy soul, content for the world to regard him as an idiot, provided that it does not make too many demands upon him.

An exchange of dialogue from this early series will demonstrate, to students and aficionados of later Goon Shows, the basic unchangeability of the Spike/Eccles character:

DEREK   Spike, I thought you had a job.
SPIKE   Da — I have — each morning I row my mudder across the river.
DEREK   Well, what's wrong with that?
SPIKE   Da — I wish I had a boat — my mudder's getting waterlogged.

Then, in a sketch about the crusades, we have:

DEREK   You there — that guard over there!
SPIKE   Da — yeah?
DEREK   Why is your uniform so dirty?
SPIKE   (*proudly*) I'm a mud guard.

There has always been a gentle, humanist side to Spike's personality. In those early days at the pub, it took the form of an avuncular attitude towards my children, Sally and James, then aged six and seven respectively. Spike would often tell them bedtime stories, and to this day they recall the adventures of the Hobbley-Gobbley men, specially created by Spike for their amusement. He also made them fearfully aware of a sinister character called 'Alfie from the Boneyard' who would subject them to unimaginable horrors if they misbehaved. If they were good, they would find little presents from the Hobbley-Gobbley men, hidden about the house. He has, of course, written books for children in latter years and has this particular interest in common with Michael Bentine, whose TV programmes and books for children are well known. This gentle and compassionate side of Spike has also shown itself in later years by his preoccupation with the preservation of flora and fauna.

During the early part of our writing association, we were, jointly and severally, as legalists put it, also concerned with providing material for Peter Sellers, who was to become the fourth member of the Goons, and an internationally-celebrated film star.

Peter Sellers was, in fact, the only member of the Goons with a show business background. His mother, Peggy Ray, came from an acting and producing family that had introduced musical revue to this country at the turn of the century. She was also descended from the famous eighteenth-century bare-knuckle fighter, Daniel Mendoza, whom Peter is alleged to resemble. Observers might possibly agree that Peter's own physical contests have been of a somewhat different nature!

His father, Bill Sellers, was a piano-playing Yorkshireman. Thus Peter's inherent acting talent was allied to an instinct for music and rhythm which found expression in his becoming a first-rate drummer. In addition, he had a superb gift for mimicry and impersonation.

By the time he was eighteen, Peter had already embarked on a showbiz career, trying himself out on stage in a theatre in Ilfracombe managed by his uncle, Bert Ray, and playing the drums in various bands before joining E.N.S.A. to entertain the troops. His application to join the R.A.F. having then been accepted, he became an A.C.2 for a while, before being seconded to Ralph Reader's R.A.F. 'Gang Show', another breeding ground for future stars.

David Lodge, the actor, a lifelong friend of Peter and fellow Gang Show artiste, recalls how Peter would borrow Gang Show costumes and appear in officers' messes at camps the show visited, disguised variously as a flight lieutenant, wing commander, and even, on one occasion, as an air commodore. His greatest coup was in India, where with darkened skin, turban and beard, he impersonated an Indian Army officer.

After the war, the trail round agents' offices began. A booking for a week of Variety in Peterborough almost ended, like Harry's in Bolton, in disaster. Peter was booed off the stage on the opening night and only the intercession of the star, Dorothy Squires, saved him from being paid off there and then. Dorothy helped him with advice and he managed to survive for the week. Soon after this he was successful at an audition for the Windmill Theatre and joined the list of stars who played there, including Harry.

The aim of all young entertainers was, of course, to appear on radio. Impatiently waiting to hear the result of an audition, Peter decided to take a short cut and rang Roy Speer, producer of the popular 'Showtime' programme. A leading comedy partnership at the time was Richard Murdoch and Kenneth Horne. It was the latter's voice that Roy Speer heard when he answered the phone. After enthusiastically recommending one Peter Sellers as an artist, the voice of Horne handed over to the voice of Murdoch to endorse this opinion. Roy was suitably impressed—until Peter's nerve gave out and he confessed his true identity. However, he'd done enough to convince Roy, who invited him for an interview. On July 1, 1948 Peter made his radio début.

That same week Harry was appearing in a programme for the 'Listen, My Children' series, produced by Pat Dixon. Both Roy Speer and Pat Dixon were to play a significant part in the process that finally brought about 'The Goon Show'.

I met Peter shortly after this and conceived a lifelong admiration for his brilliant talent. It was not just mimicry at which he excelled—his timing, his flair for comedy—all were of the highest order. Perhaps what set him most apart was his ability to give an extra comic edge to a character. In common with Spike, Harry and Michael, he possessed that sense of the ridiculous, that underlying irreverence, which was the strongest bond between them.

If Spike was the most manic depressive, Peter was, perhaps, the next, though not to the same involuntary degree. His periods of elation after a successful performance or when sharing moments of fun with his friends, were monitored by a shrewder, more pragmatic mind, as were his darker feelings of frustration. Nevertheless, he was just as susceptible to the emotional seesaw that life in show business can so easily become. Bouts of great enthusiasm and confidence would give way to pessimism and anxiety. His great comfort was his mother, Peg, whom he worshipped. She was always ready with counsel and advice, and Peter could turn to her in any situation. During the time I was writing occasional material for Peter, Peg and I had many a consultation and I came to like and admire her greatly.

Peter's one admitted weakness was an obsession with cars. As his increasing success brought greater affluence, he would buy car after car. Rather like a child seeing a glittering new toy, he would discard the old one in its favour, only to become once more disenchanted, having seen something—at least for the time being—nearer to his heart. Over a two-year period he bought and sold something like eighteen cars. He was, however, as ready to laugh about this impulsive quirk as any of us.

I was walking with him one day along Victoria Street, when he stopped in front of a well-known clothing store. There in the window was a complete outfit in cavalry twill, something not often seen. Always a trendy dresser, Peter decided on the spot that he wanted one. In we went, only to be told that there was not one in his size. Peter was annoyed. 'How dare you put something in the window that you can't supply?' he demanded. The manager apologised. 'We could get one for you from another branch, sir.' 'When?' 'By tomorrow, perhaps.'

By now Peter was well into an involuntary impression of an outraged customer. 'I don't want it tomorrow. I want it now.' 'Perhaps by this afternoon, sir?' 'No, thank you. You've already wasted enough of my time. Good day!'

With which, as the saying goes, we swep' out. I uttered words of consolation, but Peter was not to be mollified. He was in the frame of mind to acquire something, so across the road we went to Dunn's, the hatters, where Peter bought a hat. I'm quite certain he neither needed nor wanted it, but the acquisitive urge had to be satisfied. Now he could relax, and began to see the incident as the joke it was, a change of mood that was entirely characteristic.

By the end of 1949 Peter was well established as a star of radio light entertainment. Harry, with regular though not so numerous appearances, was steadily consolidating his position in programmes like 'Rooftop Rendezvous', and, joined by Mike and Peter, 'Third Division'. Spike had just completed his own series début in 'Hip Hip Hoo Roy'. It seemed to me that the stage was set to bring these talents together in one show. As yet we had not conceived a particular format, but initially I felt that a show written around Peter Sellers with the others in support would have the greatest chance of acceptance by the BBC planners.

Meanwhile, with Spike in residence, 'Grafton's' was the regular resort not only of the embryo Goons, but of many other radio and showbiz friends, among them Terry-Thomas, Jimmy Edwards, Dick Emery, Alfred Marks, Tommy Cooper, Kenneth More, Beryl Reid, Clive Dunn, Denis Norden, Graham Stark, the late Robert Moreton and others.

On occasions we would have parties after hours. Apart from the consumption of liquor and the general conviviality, a variety of games were played, among them one devised to make use of an early tape recorder I had acquired, a rather massive affair in a wooden cabinet. On this we played a form of 'Consequences', now rechristened

'Tapesequences'. One of us would murmur into the microphone the beginning of a story, unheard by the others. This would be continued by the next person, having had played back to him only the last sentence recorded by the person before. Eventually the whole story would be played back for the amusement of all. Mostly they were absurd, sometimes scatological, but usually they produced enough hilarity to make them worthwhile.

The same routine was sometimes applied to rhymes, recording one line at a time. The best and most quoted of these should be set down here in order, at least, to establish its origin:

> *'A lovely young girl from Cathay,*
> *On a slow boat to China one day,*
> *Was trapped near the tiller*
> *By a sex-crazed gorilla —*
> *And China's a bloody long way!'*

When the five of us were together, the recorder was also used to make tapes for our own amusement. I recall one spontaneously-invented 'War Report', a series of battle commentaries from various fronts together with appropriate vocal sound effects. Each time the invention flagged, we fed in a few seconds of Percy Manchester singing 'The Green Fields of England'. When we played the whole thing back, the effect was hysterical. I only wish I had kept some of those tapes.

The most vociferously inventive at the time was Michael Bentine. Bushy-haired and bearded, he probably also had the most lunatic appearance. He was fond of playing out sudden fantasies in public. Driving with Harry in the latter's ancient drophead Packhard, he would get Harry to drive very slowly and then carry on a loud conversation as though they were the pursuers in a high-speed car chase conducted by radio's popular special agent, Dick Barton. Barton's assistants, Jock and Snowy, would become Snock and Joey. Usually Harry's embarrassment would bring the chase to a speedy conclusion. Conversing in a Lyons tea-shop, Mike would suddenly drop into mock-Russian, in which he was fluently convincing, pretending he was a secret agent. In such pranks he had a willing collaborator in Peter, whose joy it was to become a different character at the drop of an accent.

Spike's fun was equally spontaneous. The best example, often quoted, was knocking on an undertaker's door, shouting 'Shop!', then lying down on the pavement with eyes closed and hands folded across his chest. Vocally, Spike almost always resorted to his favourite character, Eccles. Sometimes this was varied with a strange nasal delivery, which subsequently became the voice of Jim Spriggs, or with a hoarse, rasping voice that must have put a great strain on his tonsils.

31

This was used in later Goon Shows for an occasional character called, appropriately, Sergeant Throat. Harry, later to be the consistent character Seagoon, could also do this voice, as well as a passable imitation of Eccles. There was a time when, Spike being absent, Harry and Peter performed all the characters between them. Sometimes Graham Stark, who had become a kind of twelfth man to the team, would be called in to play additional characters.

The one accent all the Goons delighted in was a broad, almost incomprehensible Scottish, into which they would break at times to the complete bafflement of bystanders. The discovery of that strange Scots poet McGonagall (immediately rechristened MacGoonigal) has provided them with endless amusement over the years.

Variety tours sometimes included Scottish artiste Janet Brown, the clever impersonator, who worked in an evening gown. Spike would glare at her bare arms and, to her embarrassment, would shout in his broadest Scots accent, 'Get awa' frae me, ye dirty devil. Ye're showing your flesh again!'

Janet's husband, Peter Butterworth, in Variety with Harry, once stepped forward onto a somewhat insubstantial stage extension and disappeared into the orchestra pit. Harry laughed so much he had to leave the theatre to get over it. Peter got his own back when the whole company were having supper with Harry in a Cheltenham hotel. Behind Harry were double doors leading to another part of the restaurant, where a buffet reception was in progress. Peter Butterworth gave a loud knock on these doors, and Harry, not knowing what was on the other side but always ready to play games, flung them open, knocking over the buffet table which was set against them, and revealing himself to the astonished gaze of a crowd of strangers.

By 1950 it seemed to me that we had the ammunition needed to fire our ideas at the BBC. It was time to present them with an actual show. Peter Sellers, the most advanced in his radio career, obviously had to be the figurehead. To accommodate the zany characters of the others, Spike and I chose as a setting a ramshackle castle owned by 'the twenty-second (FX: SHOT. SCREAM), I beg your pardon, the twenty-*third* Lord Sellers'. To assist his impecunious lordship in raising money for the maintenance of his estate, Mike was to play a crazy inventor, while Alfred Marks was an impresario with a singing protégé, Harry. Spike was his usual Eccles character. ('Who are you?' 'I'm a serf.' 'What's that man doing on your back?' 'Da — serf-riding.') Also in the cast were Janet Brown, Peter Butterworth and Robert Moreton. The script of 'Sellers' Castle' contained a story line with a historical flashback to one of Lord Sellers's ancestors. In retrospect, the dialogue was a mixture of craziness and corn, but the whole thing had a shape and was tailored to the various talents in evidence at the time. Faith and optimism also played their part!

The package was now ready, but how to present it? From experience I knew that the participation, or at least recommendation of a reputable producer was required, and the first thing was to impress him. The vocal abilities of our friends were hardly discernible on the printed page, so a taped example of these was essential. I decided against using my own tape recorder and our own amateur production efforts. Instead, I took the cast along to a professional recording studio in Bond Street called Gui de Buire, and run by a friend of mine, Barry Barron. We only needed to record excerpts from the script, so a linking voice was required. The best man I knew for this was a fellow officer from my regiment, who was now a BBC announcer — Andrew (Tim) Timothy.

Little did Tim realise that, as a result, his dry, dispassionate, somewhat cynical tones would eventually be heard announcing the first of many Goon Shows. My favourite memory of him is as he stood, peering over his spectacles at a studio audience still giggling after a pre-show warm-up, with the admonition: 'Cease this spurious bonhomie!'

The tape completed to my satisfaction, I sought out producer Roy Speer at the BBC's Variety Headquarters in Aeolian Hall and played it to him. He was immediately interested. Could he read the script? Better still, I suggested bringing him the cast to read it to him. A few days later we crammed ourselves into the tiny Studio One in Aeolian Hall and performed the whole show for him. With a dozen of us to laugh as well as perform, the whole script sounded hilarious. 'Could you keep it up for a series?' Roy asked. Naturally we assured him we could. 'Then I'll recommend it to the planners.' We were all delighted and that evening 'Grafton's' stock of liquor was accordingly reduced.

The next step, I knew, would be the making of a 'pilot' episode of 'Sellers' Castle' for the planners to hear and approve. With a suitable audience, I thought we stood a good chance. It was with some disquiet that shortly afterwards I received the news of our appointed producer — not Roy Speer, as I had expected, but Jacques Brown, chosen because he had previously produced a 'crazy' comedy show called 'Danger, Men At Work', in which he himself had played a character called Nicholas Ridiculous.

I had nothing against Jacques personally; he was an affable, charming and amusing man. But he had a bee in his bonnet about radio comedy. He insisted it should not be necessary to use a studio audience. In vain I pointed out that listeners at home enjoyed hearing other people laugh and identified with them. More to the point, our main characters were intrinsically funny people and I had already experienced the visual impact of comic characterisation on studio audiences. We were embarking on some rather way-out comedy and needed all the help we could get. The planners might think the comedy rather revolutionary, but were bound to be susceptible to solid laughter.

After some argument, we compromised. I agreed that Jacques should make a non-audience pilot purely for our own edification, to be vetted by us and re-recorded with an audience if necessary. This was made in the BBC's Piccadilly studio. Jacques judged it successful of his own accord, and with no further reference to me, played it to the planners as it was — without an audience. Later he called a meeting which we all attended, and ruefully announced that the planners had thought the whole show too crazy and turned it down. Miserably we all filed out. Personally, I was so incensed at what I considered to be a double-cross that from that moment I never spoke to Jacques Brown again.

Over the next months, I carried on a plaintive but desultory correspondence with the BBC through Michael Standing, the reigning Head of Variety. Meanwhile Peter Sellers had acquired a new house and offered Spike accommodation of a somewhat more comfortable nature than I could provide. Here Spike brooded on the malevolence of fate, the incompetence of the BBC, and, no doubt, the failure of KOGVOS to obtain his objectives. As is so often the case, however, other factors were at work to make the dream come true.

Others influential in the BBC were aware of the four young men who were beginning to label themselves the Goons — in particular, Pat Dixon, the forward-looking producer of the early Bernard Braden shows, 'Listen, My Children' and 'Third Division' (in which he had already used Harry, Peter and Mike).

Spike was still searching for the right formula, in between bouts of depression and withdrawal, alternating with occasional music hall appearances to earn his bread and butter. Together with Peter, he taped some exchanges of Goon-like dialogue, which the latter played to Pat Dixon. Pat now prevailed upon the BBC planners to give the Goons a further chance, and proceeded to make a pilot on February 4, 1951. Perhaps feeling that the combination of an avant-garde producer and crazy comedy might take the show outside the sphere of mass entertainment, the planners now put the whole operation in the hands of one of their up-and-coming young men, Dennis Main Wilson, with whom I worked on many subsequent radio shows. He is now, of course one of BBC TV's most successful producers of comedy series.

34

Dennis joined the BBC European Service before being commissioned in the Royal Armoured Corps for the duration of the war. He was then seconded to the Propaganda Service of the Central Commission in Germany before becoming Head of Light Entertainment for the Norddeutscher Rundfunk in Hamburg. On his return to the BBC in 1947 he was eminently fitted for his first job — to audition the ex-'Stars in Battledress' and refugees from the R.A.F. 'Gang Show', either at the BBC or by seeing them perform to an audience of young ex-service people at what was then a regular show-case for them, the Nuffield Centre at Charing Cross. Many present-day stars had their first chance and a lot of good advice from the delightful lady who organized these shows, the charming and efficient Mary Cook.

Apart from his instinct for and appreciation of comedy, Dennis's other great asset was his enthusiasm, which did a great deal to sustain the spirits of all concerned. He can still quote from memory the list of stores taken on an early Goon expedition to the East Pole: 'One marble bust of Lady Astor, 240 Indiarubber Bessarabian minarets, 1047 Indiarubber Bessarabian minaret erectors and wives, 6 grand pianos, etc.' Inevitably, his affectionate and irreverent young friends soon nicknamed him Dennis Main Drain. Not only was this an obvious play on his name, but also fair comment on his predilection for sinking pints of Guinness and other brews!

By the time he was appointed to produce the Goons, he was a regular attender at 'Grafton's', in company with, amongst others, Alfred Marks and Tony Hancock, whose first individual radio shows he was also later to produce. It was through Tony Hancock, a close friend, that I was introduced not only to Dennis but also to Tony's writer, Larry Stephens, soon to join Spike and myself in the writing of 'The Goon Show'.

Larry was an ex-commando captain, who had seen some tough service in the Far East. He had a natural flair for comedy script-writing and shared with the Goons their irreverence and sense of the ridiculous, and also their artistic and musical leanings. He was both an able pianist and a meticulous illustrator of the definitive Goon character, with which he was wont to adorn the pages of his script. The original Goons from whom the name derives were big, stupid creatures in the pre-war 'Popeye' cartoons. Spike's image of a Goon was a creature with a hairy head, bulbous nose and one-cell brain, dressed in a shabby sheet and holding a barely-concealed club behind his back. The word 'goon' had been used in America of gangsters and tough guys, and R.A.F. prisoners-of-war had used it of their German guards, investing it with overtones of stupidity rather than menace (in fact, a kind of militant Eccles).

"HIP HIP HOO ROY" (6)

(THE DEREK ROY SHOW)

with

DEREK ROY
ROBERT MORETON
SPIKE MILLIGAN
CHERRY LIND
JIMMY LAVALL
THE STARGAZERS

THE DANCE ORCHESTRA CONDUCTED
BY STANLEY BLACK

SCRIPT BY: JAMES DOUGLAS AND SPIKE MILLIGAN

MUSICAL LINKS BY: JACK JORDAN

PRODUCER: LESLIE BRIDGMONT, 421 Aeolian Hall

REHEARSAL: WEDNESDAY, 9TH NOVEMBER, 1949:   3.00—6.00 p.m. PARIS CINEMA

TRANSMISSION: WEDNESDAY, 9TH NOVEMBER, 1949:   7.30—8.00 p.m. GOS/LIGHT

REC. REPS: THURSDAY, 10TH NOVEMBER, 1949:   1.30—2.00 a.m. GOS
                  SUNDAY,   13TH   "   "   12.30—1.00 p.m. GOS

REC. NO.   SOX. 30669

The title page of a November, 1949 'Hip Hip Hoo Roy' script—complete with
Spike's doodle of a Goon.

36

Larry was also a regular contributor to the humorous correspondence with which, under various pseudonyms, the Goons continued to amuse themselves and each other over the years, some of which has appeared in *The Book of the Goons*.

Spike, Larry and I now settled down to write 'The Goon Show', as we expected it to be known. However, we soon met opposition to this title from the BBC. As spokesman for the others, I found myself once more at odds with the planners, whose suggestion for a title was 'The Junior Crazy Gang'. This implicit comparison with the very popular Palladium Crazy Gang was both unapt and inept. 'Why not "The Goon Show"?' I demanded. They brushed this aside as being meaningless. The controversy continued, and the first six programmes were booked under the BBC's suggested title.

Finally, however, we compromised with the title, 'Crazy People'. Determined to have our own way, we amplified this within the programme to 'those Crazy People, the Goons', and made reference internally always to 'The Goon Show'. After the first series, the BBC gave in and our title was adopted. Even then, so the story goes, one puzzled planner was heard to ask, 'What is this "Go On Show" people are talking about?'

The shape of these programmes was somewhat different from the story-line shows of later years. They consisted of four or five unconnected sketches, separated by musical items from the Ray Ellington Quartet, The Stargazers (a close-harmony singing group), and Max Geldray, the Dutch harmonica player; accompanied by Stanley Black and the BBC Dance Orchestra.

In the first show we presented our own strange version of how the show got on the air; the story of the B.R.M.; a satire on Dick Barton; the quest for Tutankhamun; and a feature on the Festival of Britain. All, of course, highly improbable and with the aim of portraying Goon humour as we then saw it. This, as I suggested to J. P. Thomas, the noted journalist then writing for the *News Chronicle*, was 'to bring any situation to its illogical conclusion'.

I had tried to arouse as much press interest as possible in the launching of our show. J. P. Thomas responded by giving us excellent coverage in a long article published on May 17, 1951, several days before the first recording, quoting my definitions and giving a potted history of Mike, Harry, Peter and Spike. In this article a Goon was described as 'something with a one-cell brain. Anything that is not basically simple puzzles a Goon. His language is inarticulate, he thinks in the fourth dimension.' In fact, Thomas was unknowingly describing Eccles, the eternal Goon spirit! He went on to warn listeners that Goon humour was 'rather extravagant' — a remarkable understatement as it turned out.

The *Daily Graphic* wrote: 'Listeners who like it will, according to the Chief Goons, become Goons of varying degree, depending on the strength of their liking. They will be associate Goons, honorary Goons, and Goon followers.' Time has certainly proved the truth of that statement. In our subsequent individual travels around the world, we have met all three in Africa, Australia, New Zealand, the Far East, Canada, even the United States, which says a great deal to the credit of the BBC Transcription Services.

Through a friend of mine we were even able to get pictorial coverage, in the magazine *Picture Post*, of the Goons cavorting to a small audience in the living quarters of 'Grafton's'.

In the first series of 'Crazy People', Mike Bentine played the part of Captain or Professor Osric Pureheart, a zany adventurer/inventor, a character for which he was admirably suited. His inventions were normally topical subjects such as the B.R.M. (the British Racing Motors' racing car, 'so called because of its sound: Brm, Brm'), or the Brabazon (the projected national aeroplane), at which we were, as usual, taking an irreverent tilt. The launching of the 'Brabagoon' was accompanied by powerful, surging engine noises, with a puzzled Pureheart unable to take off until his voice is heard, shouting over the noise: 'Madam, will you please tell your small boy to let go of the tail!' Pureheart also dealt with the Bentine Lurgi-driven tank, the Merseygoon Tunnel, the Sydney Harbour Goon Bridge, and the launching of the Goonitania (this last being followed the next week by the *salvaging* of the Goonitania).

In a sketch based on the suggestion that the House of Commons should present a more entertaining aspect, I recall a line of Larry Stephens': 'The Foreign Secretary is now entering the Chamber, tall and erect—on his one-wheel bicycle.' The Dick Barton show was parodied unmercifully, as was the BBC itself. Any institution, in fact, was fair game. The ex-service lads were getting their own back on the establishment.

Spike was beginning to make more use of way-out sound effects, very much a feature of later shows, where whole pictures in sound were used for laughs. For example: 'Long series of smashing door down noises—goes on and on . . . give it variation in kind, i.e., first confident crashes on door with axe. These all very long. Fail—then renewed. Then furious . . then frenzied . . . then heavy, full-blooded blows . . . furious sawing . . . then hammering on door with fists . . . mad rattling of the door knob . . . then four or five heavy blows . . . then a mad furious hatchet attack on the door. . . . Door opens. Sound of hinge'—from 'The Scarlet Capsule', 2.2.59, script by Milligan.

In this first series the writing was somewhat uneven. Larry and

Spike would write some items independently; Mike would throw in ideas; I had one or two of my own and edited the whole thing. Some streamlining was bound to be necessary. Both Mike and Spike were a source of spontaneous invention, but this sometimes led to argument, which Dennis found not always easy to control.

'Crazy People' recorded its seventeenth and final edition on September 16, 1951, shortly before the General Election. This allowed us a nice twist on our obsolescent title in the final announcement, which also contained a nostalgic services flavour. The last page of script reads:

TIM   And so for the time being leave of absence is granted to those Crazy People, the Goons — Harry Secombe, Peter Sellers, Michael Bentine and Spike Milligan. Waving goodbye are the Ray Ellington Quartet, The Stargazers, temporary attachments Woolf Phillips and the Skyrockets. Passes were made out by Spike Milligan and Larry Stephens and signed by Jimmy Grafton. Dennis Main Wilson saw the party off and fainted with relief.

ORCHESTRA   UP AND HOLD TYMPS ROLL
TIM   Look out for the next forthcoming attraction.
PETER   The biggest comedy show on earth.
MIKE   The General Election, featuring —
SPIKE   Those crazy Goons —
HARRY   (*distinctly*) THE PEOPLE!
ORCHESTRA   GOONS GALLOP UP AND OUT

We were off and away.

At the end of the second series, Mike, who had other fish to fry, decided to retire from the scene. There was no acrimony, and the early friendships have been steadily maintained. However, the Milligan creative ascendancy was now firmly established. I was to continue editing the show for the next two years. Meanwhile we continued to have our 'off-duty' fun at the pub. I acquired an African vervet monkey called Johnny, whose quick eye movements and facial grimaces Spike was able to take off with uncanny accuracy — or was it the other way round? Anyway, Spike used to make the scurrilous claim that Johnny peed in the pub soup. Untrue, of course, but the little fellow did perform once from a great height on Bob Moreton's hat.

We also had a bulldog that came near to ruining Harry's sex life. But this and other stories — like that of the party where Harry conquered all comers at Indian wrestling, or the one where Mike and I shot cigarettes from each other's mouth with an air rifle, belong, as do the making of the first Goon films and so many other personal reminiscences, to a different book. The romantic lives of the Goons, all of whom were married to charming and attractive girls, as also was Larry Stephens, is their private affair. This book is intended as a record of 'The Goon Show' itself, and I will now leave its enthusiastic student and chronicler, Roger Wilmut, to analyze more closely the show's progress to its ultimate, pure Milligan form.

As I said in a recent television programme on Spike, I have always felt he has looked at the world and denounced it as idiotic, preferring instead to create and live in his own world of idiocy. 'The Goon Show' was the beginning and perhaps the most enduring part of that world. Many people have enjoyed it, but none more than those (at heart three small boys who each Sunday, for more than a decade, were let out from the school of life to run amok in the playground of their imagination.

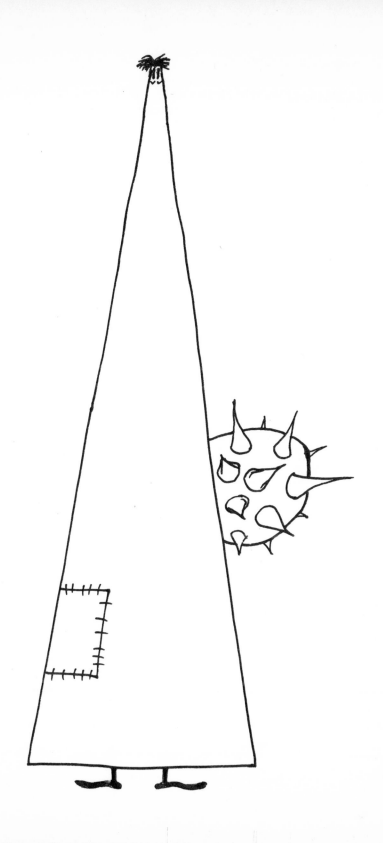

THE GOON SHOW

A Quartet of Goons

The first edition of 'Crazy People' was broadcast on May 28 1951, on London Home Service only — the other regions joined as the series progressed. The original booking for six shows was extended to a further six, and then a further five, bringing the total to seventeen.

Some familiar characters gradually emerged during the first series — Eccles, Bloodnok, Flowerdew — as well as regular characters who were later phased out — Ernie Splutmuscle, Herschell and Jones, Colonel Slocombe (a sort of American Bloodnok), and Sir Harold Porridge. Secombe emerged as a regular character, but under his own name — Neddie Seagoon was as yet some way off.

Traces of the later Goon Shows can be seen in these early sketches; already some of Milligan's favourite gags are turning up ('Please report your exact position' — 'I'm on my side with my knees drawn up' — 'Why?' — 'I'm at home in bed').

Some of the material was later re-worked — for example, 'The History of Communications' in the seventh show; and 'The Adventures of Philip String' (played by Milligan), which runs as a serial for three shows (nos. 7, 8 & 9). This latter has roughly the plot of 'Dishonoured' (5th series, later re-worked as 'Dishonoured — Again' in the 9th series), as well as a few of the gags ('Isn't the gold safe with him?' — 'Perfectly safe — wherever he and his rowing boat *are*').

As Jimmy Grafton has said, the quality of the writing and performing was rather variable. The writing ranged from brilliant to somewhat schoolboy fifth-form — Milligan was still experimenting to find his style. The others were also still developing their styles, and people who were associated with the show at that time say that it tended to be rather self-indulgent and untidy. With this type of humour there is always the danger of the cast having more fun than the audience. Dennis Main Wilson, admits that he was not, as a young and junior producer, able to exert over the show the discipline it needed. However, his enthusiasm for the Goons helped to guide the show through its early days.

The listening figures, only 370,000 for the early shows, had risen to a more respectable 1.8 million by the end of the series on 20 September. On December 26, 1951 the Goons appeared in a 45-minute Christmas pantomime — 'Cinderella', with Lizbeth Webb as the heroine. The traditional story was still recognizable, except that the Fairy Godmother was replaced by Fairy Godfather Pureheart, and Cinderella did not marry Prince Charming (Graham Stark) at the end. *Radio Times* claimed that attempts by the Goons to call the programme 'Goonderella' had been firmly resisted.

Listener-reaction to the first series seems to have been minimal — there were no letters of praise in *Radio Times*, but on the other hand, there were no complaints either. (The complaints came from *inside* the BBC.) Reaction from the Press was on the whole favourable, mostly along the lines that the show had some way to go, but was still well worth listening to; and on August 12, 1951 the Goons received the honour of being discussed by that august body, 'The Critics'.

The 2nd series began on January 22, 1952. The BBC, evidently reasoning that the damage was done by now, allowed the billing to be changed to 'THE GOON SHOW, featuring those crazy people. . . .' (Subsequent series were billed simply as 'The Goon Show'.) The BBC booked six shows, then another six, then the rest of the series, which ran to twenty-five (it would have been twenty-six, i.e., two quarters, but for the cancellation of the broadcast on 12-2-52 owing to the death of King George VI). The audience reached as many as three million for some transmissions — quite a good figure. (This, of course, was before television had made huge inroads into the listening figures.)

The format was already beginning to change. The Stargazers left after the first six shows, to be replaced by Secombe singing (straight) songs like 'Granada' and 'Ma Belle Marguerite'. The number of sketches in each programme had now dropped to four as a regularity, with a few shows having only three sketches. Harry Secombe was now emerging as a leading personality, usually featured in the first sketch. During the series he pursued Lo Hing Ding, Ho Fu Chang, the Lost Drummer, and Andrew Timothy (the show's long-suffering announcer). Secombe also masqueraded as an actor, a secret agent, a member of Military Intelligence — and was put on trial for singing. Although not yet named, Neddie Seagoon was beginning to take shape. The ever-resourceful Osric Pureheart built the Suez Canal, the Trans-Siberian Express, the Crystal Palace, Croydon Airport, the Atlantic Cable, the Channel Tunnel, and a Time Machine. Major Bloodnok was emerging as an important character and, among other things, became involved with the Blarney Stone, the Abominable

Snowman, and the Mad Mullah. Some now familiar names made their first appearance — particularly Minnie Bannister (Pureheart's Auntie), and Henry Crun, of the firm of Wacklow and Crun (Wacklow — a character that didn't last long — being played by Milligan).

For the most part the sketches were separate; towards the end of the series a few sketches ran to two episodes in one show, and on one occasion ('Crun up the Amazon'), two episodes in successive shows. However, new ground was broken in the eighth show, which was the first (apart from the special, 'Cinderella') to have a single plot lasting right through the show. Based on Rider Haggard's *She*, and entitled 'Her', it told the story of the search for She whose beauty is eternal, renewed in the everlasting flame of youth — until the man from the Gas Board came to disconnect it. It was not until the 4th series that Milligan attempted full-length stories on a regular basis, but the beginnings of the later format were already there.

All, however, was far from peaceful behind the scenes. Milligan was finding that his ideas of a comedy show did not square with those of the BBC, who considered that, having been doing it their way for years, they knew better. Long and acrimonious shouting matches ensued. Milligan, whose nerves were not steady, and hadn't been ever since he was blown up in the war, could only get what he wanted — special use of sound effects, for example — by having persistent rows. He got his own way — but at the cost of gaining a reputation for being difficult, which persists to this day. When he appeared on 'Face Your Image' on BBC-TV on 14-3-75, David Dimbleby asked him if he suffered from the prima-donna attitude that many actors have. He answered: 'I don't think so. I turn up on time, I know my lines. Dick Lester might have told you if I was a prima donna. I don't think I am. I *was* in the Goon Show days. I was trying to shake the BBC out of its apathy. Sound effects were 'a knock on the door and tramps on gravel' — that was it and I tried to transform it. And I had to fight like mad, and people didn't like me for it. I had to rage and bang and crash. I got it all right in the end, and it paid off, but it drove me mad in the process, and drove a lot of other people mad. And that's why I don't think I could be a success again on the same level, because I just couldn't go through all the tantrums.' By the end of the second series Milligan was approaching a mental breakdown.

At the end of the series Bentine and Dennis Main Wilson left the show. Bentine made a guest appearance in the 4th series, and Wilson produced one of the Goon Show 'specials'.

So far 'The Goon Show' had survived two series. Milligan was still developing, aided by Larry Stephens, the professional scriptwriter with whom he had been collaborating, and Jimmy Grafton, who had been attempting to restrain the wilder flights of fancy to the point where the audience could understand them. Stephens knew his trade thoroughly—how to construct plots (something Milligan was often a little vague about) and how to write for different types of performer. His collaboration with Milligan helped to give the show some form, where otherwise it might have stayed a collection of brilliant one-liners.

Though certainly different from other comedy shows in style, 'The Goon Show' was not as yet particularly better. If the Goons were to continue, they needed something or someone to help them over the next step on their way up. They got it in the person of their next producer, Peter Eton.

Eton had originally studied art, and worked both as a commercial artist and as a film art director before the war. When war broke out he joined the Royal Navy. Invalided out as a result of injuries received at sea, he joined the BBC in 1941, and spent some time as a features and drama producer before transferring to Variety Department in 1951.

Getting Eton was a stroke of luck for the Goons. Firstly, he had the reputation of being a hard man to make laugh, and was able to control the Goons' tendency towards self-indulgence. He made them rehearse properly and perform to a higher standard than they had achieved before—and he was not afraid to bawl them out if he thought they needed it.

The other important contribution Eton made to the show was in developing the Goons' use of radio techniques. Milligan's comment about effects being 'a knock on the door and tramps on gravel' is a little unfair, but has a certain amount of truth if it is applied to the Variety Department as opposed to the BBC as a whole. The Drama Department had by this time developed the use of realistic sound effects to a highly sophisticated art—there was a large sound effects department as well as a rapidly expanding library of pre-recorded effects. However, this sophisticated use of effects had not spread into the Variety Department and the use of effects in variety programmes was on the whole extremely limited. Even 'Hancock's Half-Hour', one of the most popular programmes of the late '50s, used them only rarely, and then they were often badly chosen and clumsily handled.

Milligan had realized the possibilities of comic sound effects; Eton's drama background provided a basis of experience in their use.

Sound effects are by no means easy to handle. Take, for example, something as simple as a door. All drama studios are equipped with an effects door, this being a full-sized door with knockers, bells, locks and bolts, usually mounted on a large box framework (to give the sound some solidity) so that the whole thing rather resembles an old-fashioned W.C. on wheels (without the plumbing). It would seem an easy matter to open and shut this door on cue — but an inexperienced spot effects studio manager can get into difficulties quite easily by mis-timing, so that the actors appear to come through the door before it's opened — or open it, exit through it, and close it, all in two seconds flat. (Try it some time.)

Another area in which Eton's drama experience helped the Goons enormously was in microphone technique. In Variety shows the artists tended to be either at the microphone, or occasionally in the distance. Drama Department had developed the use of the microphone to a fine art. It is a characteristic of most microphones, and in particular the ribbon microphones in use at that time, that if the speaker gets too close to them, his voice will become rather bass-heavy. On the other hand, as he moves back from the microphone, the ratio between the amount of sound heard by the microphone directly from his mouth, compared with the amount of sound heard as reflections from the walls and floor, will alter so that he will be *heard* to have moved back from the microphone. When an actor is correctly placed so that his voice sounds natural, he is said to be 'on-mic'; when the reverberation from the studio is heard as he moves back he is said to be 'off-mic'. This can be used to advantage to give an effect of perspective to a scene — for example, one actor can be talking on-mic (in effect, close to the listener); another can start off-mic and make an approach, so that he is heard to come in from a distance rather than just suddenly appearing.

Similarly, in a scene where several characters are talking, they can be placed at fractionally different distances from the microphone so as to emphasize the most important character, and give an impression of depth. In a drama studio, it is possible to change the acoustic (by using absorbent or reflective screens) to suggest different scenes — for instance very little reverberation for a living room (a 'dry' acoustic), or a moderate amount of reverberation, obtained by using the uncarpeted end of the studio, for a courtroom (a 'live' acoustic). Artificial reverberation can also be added to the studio sound, for a church scene for example. (The term 'echo' is often used to describe this, but strictly speaking, echo is a distinct *repeat* of sound; reverberation is a continuous dying-away of the sound.) The more subtle aspects of this changing of acoustics would not be possible in a Variety studio where there is an audience; nevertheless, the Goons managed to create remarkably vivid impressions of their imaginary locales. They were also able to use the techniques of microphone placing to help the three of them juggle the many characters in the show — for example, Sellers, playing one character on-mic, occasionally changes to another voice, moving back from the microphone before he does so, and then moving in again as he speaks the first line, so that the new character is heard to approach. This helps to maintain the illusion of there being a large number of characters present.

Most other Variety programmes never quite succeed in preventing the listener from visualizing a group of artists in a studio, whereas in 'The Goon Show' one is always able to visualize the characters in a situation — despite the fact that the scripts never take themselves seriously, and often draw attention to the fact that the show *is* taking place in a radio studio. 'The Goon Show' benefited from this drama-type training for the remainder of its existence, even after Eton had left.

The 3rd series began on November 11, 1952. Again, it was to have run to twenty-six programmes, but one was cancelled because of the death of Queen Mary.

The format of the show had changed again. Now there were three sketches, separated by only two musical items, one by Ellington and one by Geldray. The first sketch usually featured Secombe — often carrying out a crime at the bidding of a new character, the arch-criminal Moriarty, who as yet appeared only at the far end of a telephone. The second and third parts of the show were usually separate sketches, occasionally a single story in two parts — Eton was trying to persuade Milligan to write longer stories. The format, at any rate of those shows with three separate episodes, is the classic BBC Variety format — recognizable in such shows as 'Take It From Here'.

The BBC Dance Orchestra and its conductor Stanley Black, who had been with the show for the first two series, left because they were appearing in 'Educating Archie', which was being recorded on the same evening as the Goons (though not, as *Radio Times* pointed out, in the same studio — despite impressions to the contrary). Secombe was also appearing in 'Educating Archie' and the rehearsal schedule had to be arranged to allow him to record that and then come back to the Goon Show recording. The new orchestra was a group of picked session men conducted by Wally Stott, who had been arranging for the Goons since early in the first series, and whose excellent musical links gave 'The Goon Show' so much of its flavour. (Stott also wrote more conventional types of link and theme music — for 'Hancock's Half-Hour', for example — but in 'The Goon Show' he was able to break away from this and provide send-up dramatic chords and themes.)

The sketches still alternated stories of achievement and endeavour with documentaries — 'A Survey of Britain', 'Seaside Resorts in Winter', 'The Story of Civilization' (this last being a re-working of an earlier script). After only four shows, Milligan's nervous trouble, which had been getting worse all through the 2nd series, finally blew up into a full-scale nervous breakdown and he went into hospital, missing the next twelve programmes. Jimmy Grafton and Larry Stephens carried on with the scripts, though in fact after several weeks Milligan started writing again; perhaps he found it therapeutic as long as he didn't have to deal with people. (Grafton says, 'Maybe he didn't want to leave it to us!') Sellers took over Milligan's voices, and Dick Emery and Graham Stark covered alternate weeks to fill out the cast. Valentine Dyall made his first appearance with the show, and Ellis Powell (then Mrs Dale of 'Mrs Dale's Diary') made a brief appearance; thus beginning a tradition of guest appearances that was to be a feature of the later series.

Milligan returned for the seventeenth show. From then until the end of the series on May 5, 1953 only two of the shows had three separate episodes, the others having a short opening sketch and then a story occupying the remainder of the show. Several of these turned up again later. In 'The Siege of Khartoum' (no. 18, officially entitled 'The Mystery of the Cow on the Hill', which is the first episode), Major Bloodnok, besieged in Khartoum by the Mahdi, is infuriated to receive the football results instead of news of the hoped-for relief column. His complaints to Queen Victoria result in Henry Crun being sent out in charge of the Third Filth-Muck Whitechapel Fusiliers. Meanwhile Bloodnok is attempting to cope with the Intelligence Officer — Eccles. ('Eccles, you're a stupid ignorant idiot' — 'Well, I say this; I don't say much, but what I do say — don't make sense.') Eventually the relief column arrives, bringing with it the football results. This script was used again in the next series.

In 'The Man Who Never Was', Milligan presented a highly successful parody of the true story of the corpse with false identity papers and false information about the invasion of Sicily, which was left on the Spanish coast to mislead the Germans. This story was expanded and used again in the 6th series, and then again in the 8th, when it became one of the all-time classic Goon Shows.

In the twenty-fourth show the Goons conquered Everest, beating Edmund Hillary to it by a month and a day. The news of the real conquest of Everest arrived just in time for the coronation of Queen Elizabeth II. The Goons, of course, had their own version of Coronation Day; in a special programme broadcast on June 3 they presented a send-up of the BBC commentaries on the event. Here Milligan sustained a single theme through a forty-minute show.

Left to right: Jack Train, John Snagge, Tommy Handley, (BBC)
producer Pat Dixon.

Peter Eton (1944).   *Dennis Main Wilson (1958).*

(BBC)   (BBC)

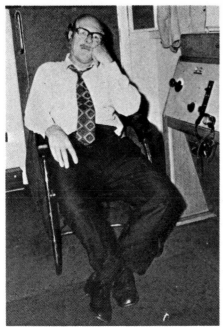

John Browell.

Wallace 'Bill' Greenslade.   (Jack M. Oakley)

The original Goons: Secombe, Bentine, Sellers, Milligan (1951).

(Keystone)

The original Goon team in Grafton's, 1951.   (Keystone)

Reunion party in Grafton's, 1969.
Left to right: Jimmy Grafton, Michael Bentine, Beryl Reid, Eamonn
Andrews, Harry Secombe, Dick Emery, Hattie Jacques, Eric Sykes.

The Goon Show team, 1953. (BBC)
Left to right: Ray Ellington, Harry Secombe, Spike Milligan,
Max Geldray, Peter Sellers.

The Goons (Secombe, Milligan, Sellers) with the Telegoons (Neddie
Seagoon, Eccles, Major Bloodnok), 1963.

(Syndication International)

The 4th series began on 2 October, 1953. Unusually, after the standard twenty-six episodes, it ran for a further four, making this the longest Goon Show series.

This series saw the final stage of the show's development into its familiar form. Two changes had taken place at the very beginning of the series, although neither was obvious to the listener. Up to this time, most of the characters—Eccles being one exception—had been indicated in the script as an instruction to the actor—for example, 'Peter (Crun)' or 'Spike (Bannister)'. For the first time, all the major characters were indicated in the script by their names—perhaps because they were beginning to take on a life of their own (which continued even after the shows had finished—see the inter-Goonal correspondence in *The Book of the Goons*).

The other change was in the recording system. Some Variety shows had always had to be pre-recorded on the Sunday prior to transmission because during the week the artists would be appearing in theatres all over the country. Up to this time, 'The Goon Show' had been recorded on slow speed disks—$33^1/_3$ r.p.m. coarse groove (i.e. same size grooves as a 78) directly cut acetate disks 16 inches in diameter; a half-hour show took three sides. Very little editing was possible, so that as far as the artists were concerned the recording might just as well have been a live transmission. With the beginning of the 4th series the shows were recorded on magnetic tape for the first time, so that mistakes, dubious ad-libs and so on could be easily edited out—and the need for exact timing disappeared because the shows could be cut to length. The Goons did not take advantage of this freedom immediately, but gradually it enabled them to take higher and higher flights of fancy, and to ad-lib at will, secure in the knowledge that anything unsatisfactory could always be removed. This gave a much greater freedom to the later shows, even though genuine ad-libs were often cut, and what sound like ad-libs were often actually in the script.

One final change of cast took place. After a few shows Andrew Timothy, their announcer since the beginning, left (he was later quoted as saying that he feared for his sanity), to be replaced by Wallace 'Bill' Greenslade. The Goons had already used Timothy as a member of the cast rather than as a straight announcer; in Greenslade they found an excellent foil, arguing with them about the quality of his announcements, passing sarcastic comments on the show in general, and eventually acting parts with them.

The first show was in the old three-episode mould; the second and third had an opening sketch followed by a story using the remainder of the show; the fourth, 'The Building of Britain's First Atomic Cannon', was a single story. It was not until the second half of the series that the shows had a continuous plot as a regular thing, but at last the dramatic format which Eton had been encouraging the Goons to adopt was working. Neddie Seagoon emerged as the hero of many adventures, aided by the characters who had established themselves in the previous series, together with some new ones — a young idiot called Bluebottle, an old idiot called Willium 'Mate', and a smooth George Sanders-type character who was to develop into the Hercules Grytpype-Thynne of the 5th series. Michael Bentine made a guest appearance in 'The Giant Bombardon', this being the last of Osric Pureheart's many inventions.

In the fifteenth show, 'The Missing Prime Minister', Sanders 'phones the police to report that Ten Downing Street is missing. Inspector Seagoon and Constable Eccles make their way there and question the duty constable, Willium ('I was tied up, Inspector, then they gagged me with this — they brought it from Ten Downing Street' — 'A hand-towel: these initials on the corner must mean Winston Churchill' — 'I 'ope so'). Bluebottle enters (to a round of applause, even this early) and is sent to have a pair of gloves, found at the scene of the crime, analyzed. He discovers that they are the sort you wear on your hands. Seagoon demotes him to Constable, much to his distress ('I shall throw myself in the river — when the weather gets warmer'). Ten Downing Street is eventually traced to France. Eccles reports that the Prime Minister has been kidnapped by the French, who have a job for him. 'Don't worry, it's a very short job' — 'What is it?' — 'Prime Minister of France!' Compared with later shows, Bluebottle sounds very odd, the voice not yet having become the falsetto noise we all love so well. Bloodnok sounds rather younger, and is as yet untroubled by his stomach upsets. The version of this story issued on a long-playing record is the 1957 re-make, under the title 'The Missing Ten Downing Street'.

The 4th (and subsequent) series scripts were no longer being edited by Jimmy Grafton, who felt this function to be no longer necessary, and after the first twenty shows Larry Stephens dropped out of the partnership, leaving Milligan standing on his own feet for the first time. He was now sufficiently developed as a writer to be able to cope on his own, and produced the stories of, among other things, the Vanishing Room, the Silent Bugler, and another attempt to climb Mount Everest — this time from the inside. The writing was still improving — and would go on doing so for some time — but with this series 'The Goon Show' at last stood in a class of its own. The longer stories allowed the characters more elbow room, and the show was settling down to the slightly slower pace (with fast patches when

50

needed) which suited Milligan's style better than the earlier rapid pacing. Four years later, when Transcription Services (of whom more anon) wanted a special series, fourteen scripts were chosen from the 4th series and re-worked (in some cases only slightly); they stood up extremely well and made a successful series under the appropriate title 'Vintage Goons'.

Another departure for the Goons during this series was contributions to other programmes. On December 25, 1953 Home Service broadcast a programme called 'Christmas Crackers' in which the casts of several current comedy series did short sketches on the subject of Christmas in general and Christmas crackers in particular — the contributions being recorded in the shows' normal sessions. The Goons were among those invited to contribute. Then, on April 2, Sellers, Secombe and Milligan were among the cast of variety artists who took part in a live programme celebrating the hundredth Boat Race.

The listening figures for the 4th series were about the same as for the previous series, varying fairly widely from show to show, but indicating a slowly-increasing popularity. The attention of the Press was attracted on a few occasions — in fact, the first single-plot show of the series, 'The Building of Britain's First Atomic Cannon', produced a bad-tempered outburst from a columnist who said he found atom bombs no fit subject for mirth (this despite the fact that, as Peter Eton wrote to point out, there were no atom bombs in the show). Then the show on December 4, 1953 included a fake announcement about an unidentified flying object proceeding across London in a westerly direction, and asked anyone who had seen it to ring a fictitious telephone number. A large number of listeners promptly tried to do just that, rather to the GPO's annoyance. Anyway, it was all good publicity.

The Goons had now completed two series with Peter Eton. He had taught them a lot about studio technique, had persuaded them into their new dramatic format (which, of course, was also the format that had served 'ITMA' so well) and, incidentally, had given Milligan a copy of Rabelais' bawdy masterpiece. This, coupled with Eton's own sense of humour (which he admits is triggered off by anything connected with dustbins or lavatories), produced a lavatorial streak which ran through the show for the rest of its life — much to the distress of BBC officialdom. The Goons had now reached the plateau which 'ITMA' occupied for most of its run — though by their own route and in their own style. Ahead of them were some of the greatest comedy performances ever broadcast.

Before the next series started, the Goons made two digressions from their normal style of programme. The first was a 'merger' with another successful comedy show, 'Educating Archie', which starred the ventriloquist Peter Brough and his schoolboy dummy Archie Andrews. 'Educating Archie' was not a particularly good programme, but it is of interest today because of the number of famous comedians who played opposite Archie at the start of their careers — Max Bygraves, Harry Secombe and Tony Hancock, among others. The series was being written in 1954 by Eric Sykes, whom Milligan knew but with whom he had never collaborated. The two decided to write a programme combining the two shows. 'Archie in Goonland', produced by Roy Speer, was pre-recorded on May 6, 1954 and broadcast on June 11. According to *Radio Times*, 'Peter Brough and Archie Andrews enter Goonland via a mousehole and are immediately involved in a fantastic adventure involving the destruction of London — and mice!' Unfortunately no recording has survived of this show, and the BBC's script has gone absent without leave, but judging by a listener's letter in *Radio Times*, the two sets of characters failed to mix. The idea of combining the Goons with another comedy programme was not tried again. The most interesting result was that Eric Sykes joined Milligan in writing most of the next series of Goon Shows.

The other experiment was rather more successful. Milligan's attention had been caught by some of the more outlandish methods used by certain city councils in attempts to free their public buildings from a plague of starlings. 'Stuffed owls, rubber snakes, ultra-violet light and high-frequency sound waves are among the dozen or more methods tried unsuccessfully in Birmingham' reported the *Manchester Guardian*. Real life was threatening to out-do the Goons. This obviously could not be allowed to pass unchallenged, and Milligan responded by writing the saga of 'The Starlings'. Instead of being presented in the usual manner in front of an audience, and with musical breaks, the programme was presented as a radio play, using the full range of drama techniques. It was also unusual in being recorded in short 'takes', which were then edited together to make up the complete half-hour programme. At that time, most radio drama was still being done live; the Goons foreshadowed the modern technique of working in sections, so that each scene can be set up, rehearsed, and recorded, before going on to the next. This simplifies many of the technical problems of a complicated drama.

'The Starlings' was broadcast on August 31, 1954 on Home Service. 'Any resemblance to a Goon Show,' said *Radio Times*, 'is due to the laxity of the producer, Peter Eton.' The story traced the attempts made to remove the luckless starlings from Trafalgar Square. Among the ideas put forward are a recording of a female starling in trouble, a recording of a female starling *not* in trouble, and, failing all else, rice puddings fired from catapults. Then the army is called in to frighten the birds away by means of noises, troops, for the use of. This device having succeeded only in deafening the entire Brigade of Guards, those responsible march through the streets clad in sackcloth. (Effect of a military band playing Chopin's funeral march, with wailing from the cast.) Then a new and brilliant idea is proposed by one Jim 'Tigernuts' Bluebottle: cover the buildings in explodable bird-lime, which can be detonated by means of sound waves, thus frightening the starlings away with the resultant bangs. Preparations are made; the artificial explodable bird-lime has to be cunningly camouflaged ('After all, the starlings know the real thing'). A suitable ceremony is laid on in Trafalgar Square ('The BBC are covering it'—'They would'). The commentator sounds remarkably like Richard Dimbleby. Speeches are made over the Great Gold Microphone of State. (This scene nearly put an end to the Goon Shows—BBC bureaucrats, who made about thirty attempts to suppress the programme during Eton's producership, on this occasion took extreme exception to Sellers's performance as the Duchess Boil de Spudswell, who sounds suspiciously like the Queen. It was largely due to the support given by senior announcer John Snagge that the series did not come to an abrupt end.)

Then comes the great moment. The explodable bird 'mixture' (as the BBC commentator insists on calling it) is detonated, and goes 'bang'. The starlings fly away. Success! True, considerable damage has been done to St. Martin-in-the-Fields; and true, too, that the starlings eventually return. However, as Seagoon points out to the House of Commons (those of them who are awake) it is obviously merely necessary to keep rebuilding, blowing up, and rebuilding. ('We'll see who gets tired first.') In any case there is a new invention to deal with the pests—rice puddings fired from catapults.

The Goons responded well to this different presentation; they were also joined by Andrew Timothy, who announced and played several small parts. The programme is very cleverly produced; the ceremony in Trafalgar Square, with the public address system going wrong, sounds particularly realistic. Unlike 'Archie in Goonland', this experiment was successful enough to merit being tried again, in 1957, when the Goons applied the same technique to the story of Cleopatra's Needle.

With the start of the 5th series on September 28, 1954 'The Goon Show' entered an important new phase. For the first time, the shows were also recorded by the BBC Transcription Services, who select the best BBC programmes (and also occasionally produce their own), and make them available to overseas broadcasting organizations. Anything likely to be of interest is transferred to processed long-playing records; overseas radio stations can then buy the right to use the programmes for a limited period — usually a year or two after issue. There is a considerable demand for BBC comedy programmes, and 'The Goon Show' is still extremely popular, particularly in New Zealand, Australia, and South Africa. These records are *not* available to the public, for contractual reasons.

Beginning with the 5th series, all Goon Shows were recorded simultaneously over landline both at Broadcasting House, for use on Home Service, and at the Transcription Services (TS) centre in Maida Vale. When the producer had made any necessary cuts to the Broadcasting House tape, removing ad-libs and so on, a marked copy of his script was sent to TS who would then cut their recording of the show to match the transmission tape. (As the original, i.e. transmission, version of the show was the responsibility of the producer, TS would not be allowed to retain anything in their copy which had been removed from the transmission version.) They would then make any cuts needed to keep the duration down to just under thirty minutes, and also remove any jokes likely to offend overseas listeners ('Ladies, Gentlemen and wogs . . . '). Later on some shows were re-issued, cut down to twenty-seven minutes to fit into a half-hour slot on commercial stations. Not every show was considered suitable — for example, some, such as 'Nineteen-Eighty-Five' were too topical, and others contained subject matter that might offend some countries — 'The Battle of Spion Kop' or 'The Terrible Revenge of Fred Fu-Manchu'. These shows were not kept, but a few which were not in the original 107 were used in the re-issues. As a result of TS' coverage of the show, the BBC has recordings of all but a few of the shows from the beginning of the 5th series onwards, although many of them exist only in the shortened versions. Most of the cuts made by Transcription Services are not particularly serious, but occasionally a good joke is either lost or garbled.

The BBC's General Overseas Service (now the World Service) had included many of the earlier shows in its world-wide 24-hour-a-day coverage in English, broadcasting them soon after their original transmissions. Overseas Goon fans had been able to hear the shows only in these short-wave broadcasts; now a large audience all over the world could follow them on local radio stations. The Goons quickly became very popular in the Commonwealth countries, and later on in the USA as well. The listening figures for the 5th series were very good, as high as $4^1/_2$ million for some first transmissions. This partly reflected the very high standard the shows were achieving, and partly the fact that, for the first time, *Radio Times* was billing the show with a sort of synopsis and cast list. These synopses were taken from the fronts of the scripts, which at this stage were being written far enough ahead to meet the *Radio Times* press date. (In later years Milligan was sometimes still writing on the morning of the recording.) The first few synopses give more-or-less accurate indications of the plots, but after that they gradually diverge from reality, as do the cast lists. This, coupled with the last-minute change when 'The Sinking of Westminster Pier' (written at Peter Eton's suggestion to celebrate the actual sinking of the landing stage near Westminster Bridge) replaced the 'The Six Ingots of Leadenhall Street', discouraged *Radio Times*; and all later series were billed simply as 'The Goon Show'.

Milligan wrote the first six shows on his own, and then the remainder of the series in collaboration with Eric Sykes. Between them they produced many classic shows in this one series — in fact the quality of the writing is more consistently high than at any other time. Nearly every show is first-class. Moriarty and Grytpype-Thynne are beginning to team up and concoct complicated plots against Seagoon. Greenslade develops an imaginary fan-club of 'Greensladers' to whom he insists on singing 'See you later, Alligator', or making appeals for money. In 'The Canal', Valentine Dyall stars as a villain who repeatedly insures his son Neddie against such unlikely events as being embedded in concrete and sunk in the canal.

A rare touch of femininity is added to the series by the appearance of Charlotte Mitchell as Maid Marian in 'Ye Bandit of Sherwood Forest':

FX	CHAINS
MARIAN	Oh, no! No! No!
GRYTPYPE	Get in there, you naughty Maid Marian.
MARIAN	Sheriff of Nottingham, take your hands off me. If they're not off in the next three hours I'll write to the police.
GRYTPYPE	Little spitfire!
MARIAN	Oh fie — oh fie — you see, my fiancé, Mr. R. Hood, will come and fisticuff you — he'll hit thee — splat, thun, blat, zowie, socko, blam, thud-biff — he learnt all his boxing from comic strips — have you ever seen a comic strip?
GRYTPYPE	Only in a Turkish Bath.
MARIAN	I don't wish to knowest that.

GRYTPYPE   In that case, good by-est.

GRAMS   **PRISON DOOR SHUTS**

MARIAN   Oh, sobs of despair—sobs!—locked in this dark dungeon with nothing but an old straw television set—this is the chamber of torture—oh woe, oh misery, oh fie, oh whatever shall I do. . . .

GRYTPYPE   *(close to mic)* The part of Maid Marian is being played by Miss Charlotte Mitchell, and a ripe little ham she's proving.

('Ye Bandit of Sherwood Forest', 28-12-54; Milligan and Sykes)

This is the show in which Sellers's famous impersonations of Sir Winston Churchill finally became too much for the BBC. In the banquet scene, Sir Winston is reputedly under the table 'looking for a blasted telegram' (a topical joke). The BBC banned any further impressions of this sort.

The Goons also investigated such unlikely mysteries as the Whistling Spy Enigma, the Phantom Head Shaver, the Dreaded Batter-Pudding Hurler, the Lone Banana, and the Booted Gorilla.

The fifteenth show of the series is particularly interesting. Called 'Nineteen-Eighty-Five', it was inspired by the television dramatization of Orwell's *1984*. The play had caused a furore, largely on account of the brain-washing sequence near the end—this was the first time that television had brought anything unsettling into people's homes. Milligan and Sykes wrote a brilliant parody of Orwell's book, working in terms of the 'Big Brother Corporation' and Independent Television, which had not yet begun operations but was the subject of a great deal of discussion.

The plot of 'Nineteen-Eighty-Five' stays remarkably close to the original, nearly every major scene having its counterpart. Even the controversial brain-washing sequence has its parallel. In the original, Winston Smith is taken to 'Room 101' to face 'the worst thing in the world'—in his case, rats. In the Goons' version, Seagoon is taken to 'the listening room'—and exposed to the opening music from 'Mrs. Dale's Diary', 'Life With the Lyons' and 'Have a Go!'. His collapse is immediate.

The show was so well received that the Goons repeated it five weeks later—not a recorded repeat, but a new performance of the same script. (It was recorded on the same day as another show, so it saved the writers from having to produce two scripts in one week.) This time John Snagge read an announcement for them (recorded a few days earlier)—the first of a number of pre-recorded appearances he made over the years.

Once again 'The Critics' examined a Goon Show—this time

'China Story', the history of an attempt to assassinate the Chinese General Kash-Mai-Chek. The tradition of parodying well-known books continued with 'Under Two Floorboards', which was based loosely on *Beau Geste*. One of the Goons' best-remembered plots is 'The White Box of Great Bardfield', in which British snow, exported to the Sudan, is found to have melted; the resultant water is further exported to the Sahara, but has of course evaporated; however, the cardboard boxes used for transporting the invisible export can be re-cycled by returning them to Britain, where there is a need for boxes in which to ship snow to the Sudan. . . .

The popularity of the show during this series was tremendous. Eton's discipline and encouragement and Sykes's co-authorship had resulted in the shows being tightly constructed with logical plots, well paced, technically very well produced, with strong individual characters against a background of fantasy and satire. Many people still regard this as the Goons' best period, perhaps because there was still a just-recognizable relationship to the more conventional comedy programmes. This of course must be a matter of individual opinion, but those who were prepared to make the effort to keep up with Milligan's mental processes were rewarded by hearing the boundaries of comedy pushed back further than ever before.

With the 6th series, the Goons, having had the experience of working in a highly disciplined manner, were now beginning to relax again. However, with the experience of the 4th and 5th series behind them, they now knew exactly when to keep one foot on the ground, and when to take flight.

Sykes co-wrote only three shows in this series. Milligan was now fully confident of his ability to handle strong story ideas, and was able to stand back from the story line to allow some of the characters—particularly Bluebottle and Eccles—to play scenes which developed their characters rather than the plot. Having learnt the rules of script construction, Milligan was not going to be restricted by them.

The 6th series began on September 20, 1955. The first three scripts were rather weak, but with 'Napoleon's Piano' and 'The Case of the Missing C.D. Plates' the previous high standard returned. The confidence-trick worked by Grytpype-Thynne and Moriarty on Seagoon in the latter programme is one of the most complex yet: Neddie has been struck down in his prime by a piano—of course, if the offending instrument had been wearing C.D. plates, it would have enjoyed diplomatic immunity, so that Seagoon could not sue it. He is therefore inveigled by Grytpype into screwing C.D. plates onto the piano under cover of darkness, thereby ruining his chances of getting damages.

57

The series continued with some more classic shows—the story of Rommel's treasure (which was buried several feet above ground), a parody of *Lost Horizon*, and the Saga of the International Christmas Pudding. A fifteen-minute 'special' was broadcast in 'Children's Hour' on December 8, 1955. Then, on December 20 came a starring part for Greenslade. 'The Greenslade Story' tells the tale of a common-or-garden BBC announcer who rises to unheard-of heights of popularity; so much so that the public demands to see him in the flesh ('What, *all* of it? He's a danger to shipping'). The BBC, faced with a persistent announcer-kidnapping campaign by Grytpype and Moriarty, sends John Snagge to plead with Greenslade not to desert them. Snagge, who for once is present and not pre-recorded, reads his part in his best 'here-is-the-news' voice.

FX	KNOCKING: DOOR OPENS
ELLINGTON	*(African chief)* Thou knocked?—Oh shiverin' white infidel, cor blimey.
SNAGGE	Yes, is Wallace in?
ELLINGTON	Wall-ace? Dost thou mean the Great Greenslade? He whose voice drips like honey upon the ears of the waiting world—he of the velvet-petalled tongue?
SNAGGE	Yes—yes, that's Wal.
ELLINGTON	Who shall I say craves audience?
SNAGGE	Tell him it's John Snagge—no, no, wait—tell him it's Snaggers—he whose voice once yearly rings out from the Thames motor-launch (that usually fails)—he whose voice tells the masses of a watery combat 'twixt men in two slender willow-slim craft, that race on the bosom of our river and race past Mortlake brewery towards their Olympic goal.
ELLINGTON	Cor blimey, man, follow me.
SNAGGE	Dear listeners—I was led across a marble courtyard of solid wood—and here and there silver fountains gushed claret. And there, there, lying in a silken hammock suspended between two former Television Toppers, was Wallace Greenslade.
GREENSLADE	Ah, John, dear John. You couldn't have arrived at a better moment. I was just about to unveil a small bronze statue of myself.
SNAGGE	Now look here, Wallace—there's a rumour going round the Corporation that you're thinking of leaving.
GREENSLADE	Well, John, I have been getting offers.
SNAGGE	But Wallace—you're not going to leave us? Remember, you're British.

58

GREENSLADE	Dear John — what can I say?
SNAGGE	What's the matter, Wallace? Aren't you happy with us — isn't three pounds ten a week enough?
GREENSLADE	Not quite, John.
SNAGGE	But, man alive, you've a free copy of the *Radio Times* every week —
GREENSLADE	Yes, there is that.
SNAGGE	Well, now look, Wallace —
GREENSLADE	What, John?
SNAGGE	I've been given authority to offer you *four* pounds a week — and you can read the nine-o'clock news at half past if you want to — *and* take your own time about it.
SEAGOON	Not so fast, Mr. John Boatrace Snagge.
SNAGGE	That voice came out of a little ball of fat that sprang from behind a piano-stool.
SEAGOON	My name is Neddie Seagoon.
SNAGGE	What a memory you have.
SEAGOON	Not so fast.
SNAGGE	I said it as slowly as possible.
SEAGOON	So — you're the famous John Snagge, eh? Known as the male Sabrina of Portland Place.
SNAGGE	Now steady, Seagoon, or I'll ban your record on 'Housewives' Choice'.
SEAGOON	Ahem! Never mind — I still have my shaving turn.
GRAMS	WHOOSH
GRYTPYPE	Mr. Snagge — I fear you have arrived too late to save Mr. Greenslade. He has already signed a theatrical contract at five pounds a week.
SNAGGE	*(horror)* Five pounds? There *isn't* that much!
GRYTPYPE	Yes, there is — and here it is, in used stamps.
SNAGGE	*(sad)* Alas — I cannot offer him more. So this, then, is the end of the once-great BBC announcing staff.
ORCHESTRA	SOLO MUTED TRUMPET — PLAYS 'LAST POST' UNDER NEXT SPEECH
SNAGGE	Where are they now, that noble band? Andrew Timothy — missing; Alvar Lidell — went down with his lift; Richard Dimbleby — overweight; and finally, Ronald Fletcher — gone to the dogs.
SEAGOON	Stop — stop — you're breaking my heart. I can help you — I have a man here to take their place. Speak, lad, speak!
ECCLES	Winds light to variable. Wait a minute, Mr. 'Nagge — you're very lucky to get me.
SNAGGE	I have no choice. Put him in a sack.

('The Greenslade Story', 20-12-55; Milligan)

Alas, Eccles too succumbs to the lure of the bright lights and five bob a week, and supplants Greenslade as a popular idol at the Palladium. The BBC is left with only one faithful announcer — Bluebottle.

The International Christmas Pudding makes a return appearance, this time in the story of a dastardly raid on the recipe; so does Charlotte Mitchell, in 'Tales of Montmartre'. Valentine Dyall appears in 'The House of Teeth' as Doctor Longdongle, who collects false teeth to make castanets for his beloved. One of the all-time classic Goon Shows is 'Tales of Old Dartmoor'. This was included on the first long-playing record of the shows, released in October 1959; it tells the story of the removal of Her Majesty's Prison, Dartmoor, to the south of France, leaving in its place a full-sized cardboard replica. 'Tales of Old Dartmoor' was the last show produced on a regular basis by Peter Eton, who left the BBC and defected to Independent Television. He had given the Goon Show a great deal, and his influence was to stay with them in the remaining series; even though they went through a difficult period during which their standard declined, they never lost the grasp of radio techniques he had given them.

Produced by Pat Dixon

The show's next producer, Patrick Kenneth Macneile-Dixon, had been an advertising executive associated with commercial broadcasting from Radio Normandie, one of the pre-war stations following in the steps of Radio Luxembourg. He wrote some scripts for the BBC, mostly connected with his great interest in jazz, and eventually joined the Corporation early in the war. He had given much encouragement to the young Goons in the days when they were struggling to get their ideas on the air, but had not produced 'Crazy People' because he had been too busy with other programmes.

Pat Dixon stayed with the show for the remainder of the 6th and for the 7th series. He kept the programme on a looser rein than Peter Eton had, which at first was beneficial. Having learnt discipline, the Goons were beginning to expand their ideas, and a less rigid framework was helpful to them. The remainder of the 6th series produced 'The Fear of Wages', 'The Man Who Never Was' (expanded from the 3rd series show), and 'Scradje', in which John Snagge (prerecorded) joined the rest of the population of the British Isles in carrying a gas-stove above his head in order to prevent his boots from exploding.

'The Great Tuscan Salami Scandal' is of interest because of the absence of Geldray, Ellington and the orchestra owing to a musicians' strike. The musical links were provided by Milligan in the guise of one

Adolphus Spriggs (a non-playing musician). The audience was also treated to a rendition of Milligan's soulful ballad 'I'm Walking Backwards for Christmas', with piano obbligato by Sellers.

The Goons contributed a five-minute item to a celebration of St. David's Day, broadcast in the Light Programme on March 1, 1956. Entitled 'The Goons Hit Wales', it briefly examined the history of that country, ending with a version of 'We'll Keep a Welcome'. With commendable tolerance the Welsh refrained from starting a war.

The series ended on March 20, apart from the transmission two weeks later of 'The Pevensey Bay Disaster', postponed from November 22 because a train crash in the plot made it unsuitable at the time, there having been a rather serious one at Didcot on the day of the recording.

On August 24, the Goons invaded the annual exhibition, the National Radio Show, which in those days was a major event in the world of broadcasting. They recorded a new production of 'China Story' in the special studio at Earl's Court, with Dennis Main Wilson in charge. The performance is in fact slightly better than the original version of twenty months earlier; the script is identical. However, the 5th series performance was the one chosen for issue in 1968 on a long-playing record.

The 7th series began on October 4, 1956. Peter Eton produced the first two programmes, returning briefly to the BBC to do so, and then Pat Dixon took over for the remainder. Larry Stephens had returned to help Milligan with the writing. The series got off to a flying start with 'The Nasty Affair at the Burami Oasis', involving the English and Arab football teams and an oasis full of gin. Valentine Dyall appeared in the second show, 'Drums Along the Mersey', and again in 'The Spectre of Tintagel', the fifth show. The sixth show, 'The Sleeping Prince', was postponed until later in the series because its Latin-American-type revolution was too touchy a subject in view of the Hungarian uprising. In 'The Great Bank Robbery' the cast sing along with the closing signature tune — a musical experience which defies description.

Transcription Services recorded a special show for their own use — 'Robin Hood'. This has some stretches of script in common with 'Ye Bandit of Sherwood Forest', and features Valentine Dyall as the Sheriff of Nottingham, and Dennis Price (who seems a little out of place) as Prince John. There was no Maid Marian this time, and much of her part was given to Bluebottle. The show was issued on a gramophone record in 1971. Another special show, called 'Operation Christmas Duff', was recorded on December 9 for the General Overseas Service, who broadcast it on December 24 and 25; it was aimed principally at British troops abroad.

Meanwhile the series continued. The Goons held their own version of the popular TV panel game 'What's My Line'; installed a telephone at 17a, Africa, the home of the inventor of the *black* telephone; and visited the London of Samuel Pepys for 'The Flea'. Listeners were assured that no real fleas were used in the programme, their parts being taken by small grasshoppers painted black.

The style of the show was relaxing — perhaps a little too much. On the credit side, the plots became wilder and less tightly constructed, which enabled Milligan to explore more fully the strange world and characters he had created. Long scenes which did nothing to carry the plot forward — or indeed in any direction — were included, often between Bluebottle and Eccles. These provided some classic moments, with the audience (and Secombe) in hysterics. Inevitably, this exploration of the possibilities of Goonery produced a higher proportion of shows or sequences that did not quite come off than in the earlier two series; this seems a small price to pay for the development in Milligan's writing.

However, if Dixon had a fault it was that he was too nice a person. The Goons still needed *some* discipline, particularly as they were by now so good that they were finding rehearsals a bit of a bore. By the time the show was recorded, it had been read through, corrected, 'walked through' at the microphone, and then had a full-scale rehearsal. All through this the Goons would be making asides, in-jokes, and generally amusing themselves. When it came to the recording, many of these remarks were included in the performance. Once again there was the danger of the cast having more fun than the audience. The trouble is not too apparent in the 7th series — it was in the 8th that it got a bit out of hand — but the beginnings of the bad habit can be heard towards the end of Pat Dixon's producership. Possibly the cast's brandy-and-milk in the back room had a little to do with it (those cries of 'round the back for the old brandy' before the musical items are not there just for effect!).

Still, on balance, Dixon allowed the Goons a freedom to develop that led eventually to the peaks reached in the 9th series. The end of the 7th series has a number of excellent shows. Neddie was persuaded to insure the English Channel against catching fire in 'Insurance, the White Man's Burden', which also brought a running gag about penguins to a head by including a penguin singing at the piano — an amazing squawking noise ('and them's all 'is own words, too, Mate'). Bernard Miles brought his best rustic accent to 'The Rent Collectors', which also marked the first appearance of the character Little Jim. Jack Train brought Colonel Chinstrap to visit his junior officer Major Bloodnok in 'Shifting Sands', emphasizing the debt the Goons owed to 'ITMA'.

62

The twenty-second show, 'The Africa Ship Canal', was inspired by the closure of the Suez Canal after the Suez crisis in 1956. Owing to the canal being closed, British aeroplanes are having to fly round the Cape. Seagoon proposes to dig a canal across Africa so that the planes can fly over it. In order to safeguard against accident, there is to be no water in the canal.

The last programme of the series was a resounding success — 'The Histories of Pliny the Elder', issued on a gramophone record in 1974. The Romans invade Britain, immediately finding themselves involved in a game of football. Caractacus Seagoon is sold as a slave to the Coliseum, meeting Brittanicus Bloodnokus there. ('You know that saying, "Caesar's wife is above suspicion"? Well, I've put an end to all that rubbish!')

Pat Dixon left the show at the end of this series, partly because of the onset of the cancer from which he died, while training as a television producer, in October 1958. He was a great loss to broadcasting. He was also a great loss to the Goons, who now found themselves without a regular producer.

Producers all in a Row

Before the 8th series started the Goons repeated the experiment of 'The Starlings', using the radio play format again. 'The Reason Why' was produced by Jacques Brown, whose only previous contacts with the Goons had been the 'Sellers' Castle' fiasco in their pre-Goon days, and one programme in the 4th series. 'The Reason Why' was recorded on August 11, 1957, and broadcast on the 22nd. The result was not as effective as 'The Starlings', partly because the story chosen, that of the bringing of Cleopatra's Needle to England, was based firmly on reality and so the Goons could never really take flight. There was also less scope for the sort of complicated sequences that had made 'The Starlings' so interesting. The programme is amusing — particularly the musical fill-up at the end — but not outstanding.

The 8th series began on September 30, 1957. Charles Chilton produced the first five programmes, Roy Speer the next nine, Tom Ronald the next two, then Chilton returned for the remaining ten.

Tom Ronald frankly did not like the Goon Show; Roy Speer, who had given Sellers his first chance in 1948, was more in sympathy with them but, not being in good health and in any case near retirement, was prepared to let them carry on more or less uncontrolled. Chilton managed rather better, and most of the best shows from this series were produced by him, but he was not really at home with this sort of production. He had previously written and produced 'Riders of the

Range' and 'Journey into Space'. The latter, with its hero Jet Morgan, had been one of radio's most successful ventures into science fiction. 'The Goon Show', however, was a little out of his field. To complicate matters, Transcription Services arranged a series of fourteen shows for their own use, these being recorded on the same evenings as some of the eighth series shows. Although this special series consisted entirely of re-vamped fourth series scripts, it meant an increased load on Milligan, who, even with Stephens's help, was finding the writing a strain.

The shows in the 8th series vary tremendously in their quality. At their worst they are really very messy. The cast are obviously enjoying themselves hugely, but the in-jokes and lack of discipline tend to make the listener feel rather left out of it. There is far too much reliance on catchphrases and references to past shows which are only intelligible to someone who has been following the programmes very closely. On several occasions effects sequences, which to be really funny should be logically controlled in the manner Eton had taught them, come apart at the seams.

Even so, there are some brilliantly funny shows. 'The Burning Embassy' has a convoluted plot involving the British Embassy in China, as well as a very odd auction ('Sold to the gentleman who keeps changing his voice').

In 'The Treasure in the Tower', Milligan seems to have set out to see just how complicated he can make the plot, which takes place simultaneously in two different periods of time. In 1600, Sir Walter Raleigh (Seagoon) and Eccles set off for home from the Americas with a treasure which they hope to smuggle into England. In 1957, Neddie Seagoon hires Grytpype and Moriarty to dig at the Tower of London, in the hope of finding buried treasure. They succeed only in finding the Crown Jewels. Meanwhile, in 1600, Raleigh and Eccles are planning to bury the treasure in the Tower of London. Sailing up the Thames (in 1600), they are fired at by Major Bloodnok (in 1957). Discovering (in 1600) that they have forgotten to bring the treasure with them, Raleigh sends Eccles back for it. Eccles arrives in 1957 by mistake, with the treasure. He returns to 1600 with it, thus being unable to help Bluebottle who, having been slung into the Thames (in 1600) by Raleigh, is drowning (in 1957). Meanwhile (in 1957), Seagoon has hired archaeological organists Crun and Bannister to continue the digging. They fail to find any treasure, and leave a 30-foot hole by the tower. It is in this hole that Raleigh buries the treasure (in 1600), which is why it wasn't there when the hole was *dug* (in 1957). (Is that all quite clear?)

'African Incident' is a parody of *The Bridge on the River Kwai*, following the plot very closely, and providing the opportunity for

Sellers to give a highly realistic impression of Alec Guinness. Cécile Chevreau also appears in this show, in a romantic interlude with Major Bloodnok. 'The Thing on the Mountain' starts with the terror of a Welsh village at the unearthly noises coming from the top of a nearby mountain. Seagoon investigates, to find Minnie and Henry calling the elephants in with an old bugle. ('Elephants? These are chickens!' — 'No wonder they wouldn't lay!') But of the monster there is no sign. Greenslade comments — as he often did — 'It's all in the mind, you know'.

The writing had been divided between Milligan and Stephens up to now. 'The Thing on the Mountain' is credited to Larry Stephens and Maurice Wiltshire, although Milligan must have contributed at least a few ideas to it. A few weeks later, after Wiltshire and Stephens had collaborated on 'The White Neddie Trade', Stephens dropped out. He appears once more in the credits, with a script polished up by Maurice Wiltshire, in the 9th series, but his collaboration on 'The Goon Show' effectively ends with 'The White Neddie Trade'. His health was failing, and he died a couple of years later. As a professional script-writer, well versed in his craft, he had been a great help to Milligan. He had even been able to write remarkably good pastiche Milligan when necessary: Milligan, suffering as he was from the nervous strain involved in writing the shows, had on occasions been unable to contribute very much to the script.

For the twenty-first show, an old script was revived — 'The Man Who Never Was'. This had first appeared in the 3rd series, and had then been expanded for re-use in the 6th. Milligan now made slight alterations to it, principally writing in two characters who had appeared only recently — the Indian gentleman Lalkaka and Banerjee. He also improved the ending. The show tells the story of an uncooked German boot found washed up on the English shore. In it are the microfilmed plans of a German secret weapon. Seagoon makes arrangements for the Woolwich Arsenal to build it from the plans, in order to find out what it is. Meanwhile Major Bloodnok is interrogating a German prisoner. ('I'm not a spy, I'm a shepherd' — 'Ah, shepherd-spy!') Minnie and Henry arrive with the brilliant idea of having Field Marshal Montgoonery (Eccles) washed ashore on the enemy coast with a copy of the microfilm in his pocket (in order to fool the Germans into thinking that the British *haven't* got the plans). Before Henry can explain himself, the cast get rather off the script — so much so that Minnie has to prompt Henry, Sellers having lost his place ('Line fourteen' — 'I wondered where we were'). Eventually the secret German weapon is constructed and tested. It turns out to be a barrel-organ. ('Don't waste it — Eccles, up on the top and start scratching — Secombe, the tin mug, and off we go!').

It is interesting to compare the 6th and 8th series versions of this script. In the two years separating them the Goons had extended their technique, and the later version is better in every way, the lines being much better delivered and the slight alterations to the script having made a tremendous difference. This is one of the best of all the Goons' performances; even the muddle that they get into during the Minnie and Henry sequence, giggling, ad-libbing, and losing their place in the script, for once does not detract from the overall effect. It is a great pity that Transcription Services, having issued the earlier version, decided to ignore this much better performance. Fortunately there is an uncut transmission version in Sound Archives.

The next show, 'World War One', contains some of the most complicated sound effects sequences yet, foreshadowing the highly complex use of effects in the next series. One of the high spots is the sudden flowering in Eccles of a romantic attraction to Major Bloodnok ('My little darling. I want you to have these, I picked these for you. I grew them myself' — 'A handful of hair — how sweet! Singhiz, put these in a jar of hair-oil').

The twenty-fourth show, 'Tiddleywinks', was inspired by a real-life tiddleywinks match in which the Goons had been involved. The Cambridge University tiddleywinks team had challenged the Duke of Edinburgh to a match; he nominated the Goons has his champions. Nothing loth, the Goons entered the fray. They lost. In 'Tiddleywinks', Seagoon, having been cheating, is hauled up before John Snagge ('You've been a cad, Seagoon. Your conduct as a Royal Champion has been disgraceful. I must ask you, formally, to hand back your tiddleys').

The next show, 'The Evils of Bushey Spon', was reduced to total chaos by the inclusion of A. E. Matthews as guest star — for the latter part of his career he always refused to be bound by mere details like the script. He appears in the last few minutes; Milligan wrote the script with blank lines for Matthews, knowing that he wouldn't read any lines he was given, but in the event Matthews refused to stay anywhere near the plot, and the entire end of the show was ad-libbed by all concerned. This show was unavailable for many years, but during 1975 BBC Records persuaded Transcription Services to exhume their copy from the vaults, and the programme was issued on a long-playing record.

The series came to an end on March 24, 1958 with 'The Great Statue Debate'.

The special series for Transcription Services that had been recorded concurrently with the 8th series was rather more successful, principally because the scripts, having been carefully chosen from the 4th series, were mostly very good. The amount of re-working applied to them varied — 'The Dreaded Piano Clubber', for example, had originally been only one episode, and so had to be expanded to three times its original length. On the other hand, 'The Albert Memorial' was only slightly altered from its original appearance as 'The First Albert Memorial to the Moon'. In 'The Giant Bombardon', which had originally been written to include Bentine, some of his part was taken by Valentine Dyall, the rest being spread among the other characters, principally Seagoon. Six of these shows were broadcast on Home Service immediately prior to the 9th series; unfortunately *Radio Times*, in a badly worded write-up, managed to give the impression that these were recorded repeats of 4th series shows. The remaining 'Vintage Goons' have still never been broadcast in this country.

This had been a very difficult period for the Goons — the chopping and changing of producers had been very bad for the show. Luckily the next producer turned out to be as fortunate a choice for the Goons as had Peter Eton in 1952.

With Browell to the Peak

At the end of the 8th series, Milligan was understandably very annoyed about the producer situation, and complained bitterly to Jim Davidson, then head of Variety Department. Milligan demanded that Bobby Jaye, who had been the studio manager for the last three series, and with whom Milligan had been getting on very well, should produce the next series. Obviously Jaye could not produce the show, as he had had no official training as a producer, but he was asked to suggest a suitable alternative. He pointed out that John Browell, who at that time was a fairly junior producer in Variety Department, had been the studio manager on three of the earlier series under Peter Eton, and would be ideal. At first this suggestion was rejected on the grounds that Browell was too junior, but in the end he was appointed. He was an excellent choice. His experience with the Goons went right back to the first few editions of 'Crazy People', which he had studio managed under Dennis Main Wilson. He left because he didn't get on with Wilson, and returned soon after the beginning of the 3rd series because other studio managers were finding Eton too much for them. He stayed with the show until the end of the 5th series, when he left to become a producer.

Browell was able to combine an understanding of Goon humour with the tight control that the show now badly needed. Under his direction the pace was considerably speeded up, as were the effects — particularly now that tape could be used to provide rapid editing. He edited the recordings more tightly to remove any

bewildering ad-libbing, and encouraged the Goons into a much more controlled and effective style.

The 9th series began on 3 November, 1958 directly following the six 'Vintage Goons'. The standard of writing varied, but the best programmes in this series show Goon humour at its most brilliant. Milligan's own system of logic, which usually involved leaving out several essential steps of reasoning on the way to a conclusion that seemed correct if inexplicable, was almost fully developed by now. The listening audience was smaller than it had been a few series earlier, those who could not keep pace with Milligan having given up. The figures for the Home Service transmissions were around the one million mark, many of these being highly enthusiastic regular listeners.

Milligan wrote most of the series on his own. The first show, 'The Sahara Desert Statue', examines the effect of an atomic explosion upon a nude Welshman holding a rice pudding. 'I was Monty's Treble' reveals the story of the impersonations of Field Marshal Montgomery. 'The £1,000,000 Penny' returns briefly to the format of the 3rd series, with a murder mystery which is solved during the first musical item, leaving the remainder of the show to the story of the rich penny, left a million pounds in a will. In 'The Pam's Paper Insurance Policy' an offer by the editor of Pam's Paper to pay one thousand leather pounds to the next of kin of anyone found drowned in water, provided that a copy of Pam's Paper is found on the deceased body, results in a spate of people being heaved into the Thames—to the delight of Little Jim, who had appeared with his catchphrase 'He's fallen in the wa-ter' in the 7th series.

'The Seagoon Memoirs' is mostly pastiche Milligan, being written by Larry Stephens and Maurice Wiltshire—however, the result is quite successful. 'Queen Anne's Rain' deals with the very British subject of rain. It is 1880 and the rain has been falling for forty days and forty nights (making a grand total of eighty days and nights). The floods are rising at three-and-sixpence an hour. The villagers of Upper Dicker are convinced that it is all Queen Anne's Rain. Grytpype and Moriarty persuade them that the sky is leaking, which is why the rain is coming in. ('What proof have you?'—'Water-proof!')

The eleventh show of the series, 'Who Is Pink Oboe?', is remarkable in that Sellers developed throat trouble shortly before the recording and was unable to go on. Browell managed to replace him in the two hours available—with Valentine Dyall, Kenneth Connor, Graham Stark, and Jack Train. Connor plays Willium and Sydney Mincing, the character from 'Ray's a Laugh' that had been parodied by Sellers in a number of shows ('You know, I don't feel strange in this programme at all'). Dyall replaces Grytpype-Thynne, and fights a duel with Moriarty—the 'Miserere' at ten paces. Train once again plays Colonel Chinstrap. The script was hurriedly altered to accommodate these changes, and the result is quite effective.

The next show was 'The Call of the West', which is the culmination of all the Goon Show's techniques. It is fast-paced and brilliantly funny, although probably it would be totally incomprehensible to anyone not familiar with the Goons. Colonel Slocombe, the hero of many first and second series adventures, reappears as the commander of the U.S. 9th Cavalry. The dreaded Nobblynee Indians pursue Eccles, shooting at him ('But I just stuck my tongue out at 'em'—'Get wounded?'—'Yer'—'Where?'—'In the tongue'). Grytpype and Moriarty are discovered selling saxophones to the Indians. Slocombe's aide, Lootenant Hern-Hern, takes a dim view of this as they are causing unemployment among white musicians. Bluebottle arrives, having walked most of the way from Finchley, and gets involved in a game of poker. The show is further enlivened by the sudden (and only) appearance of his mum, played by Secombe, who drags him off home. Finally Minnie and Henry steel themselves against the approach of the marauding Indians ('Are they the ones that commit atrocities?'—'Yes, Min'—'I'll go upstairs and get ready').

The following show is almost as brilliant. Milligan not having been able to produce a script that week, Browell chose a 5th series script—'Dishonoured, or The Fall of Neddie Seagoon'. Re-titled 'Dishonoured—Again', it was performed with very few changes to the original text. As with 'The Man Who Never Was', the cast gives a much better performance the second time round. Every line is delivered to its best advantage, the pace is excellent, and the plot a strong one. Seagoon is discovered sharing an Embankment bench with Eccles ('Christmas Eve and still no offers of Pantomime'). Moriarty and Grytpype offer him a post in a bank, looking after the gold. The temptation is too much for him, and he decamps with it—joined, to his surprise, by Grytpype ('There's no point in staying, there's more money in the van than there is in the bank'). They set sail, but Neddie is tricked into thinking that Moriarty has gone off on his own with the gold, and rather rashly dives off the ship in pursuit ('Ten miles he swam. The last three were agony'—'They were over land'). Having collapsed in a heap, he is discovered by Minnie and Henry, who are out for a drive ('Put the brake on, Min'—'It doesn't suit me, Henry'). Recovered, he makes his way ιo a den of vice in the Indian Quarter of Bombay, where he watches the sensuous Dance of the Seven Army Surplus Blankets. Underneath them is Eccles. ('Eccles! You're not a woman!'—'I know that! But don't tell the manager'—'Why not?'—'We're engaged!') They join the army—under Major Bloodnok. ('I want a chance to prove that I'm a man!'—'Report to the M.O.')

Finally Neddie gives his all in battle with the Red Bladder. ('Seagoon fought like a madman—how else?') On that spot is now a little white stone. Once a year Min lays flowers on it. ('I haven't the heart to tell her that, roughly translated, it says—Bombay, forty-nine miles.') This show was included on the first long-playing record of Goon Shows, together with 'Tales of Old Dartmoor'.

The series continued with another highly successful programme—'The Scarlet Capsule', which was a parody of the BBC Television serial 'Quatermass and the Pit', a high tension thriller by Nigel Kneale. This was another show to be issued on a gramophone record.

The series ended on February 23, 1959 with 'The £50 Cure'. Secombe was in bed suffering from mumps. He sent a message to the others: 'Sorry. Unable to appear tonight. Peruvian Crut has struck again. Don't drink all the brandy. Love from Tumescent Tom, alias Ned.' His place was taken by Kenneth Connor, and the show made a rather muted end to the series.

It had been intended by both the Goons and the BBC that this should be the last of the Goon Shows. Milligan told Paul Tanfield of the *Daily Mail*: 'I don't know what I shall do now. With my three children I could draw £6 a week from the Finchley Labour Exchange. That'll be enough for us to live on, if I can persuade my wife to give up her luxurious tastes—such things as soap.' More seriously, he said, 'The show was starting to degenerate. It had to come to an end.'

The fans, however, were not prepared to give up the show without a struggle. At the end of the recording session a group of girls filled the foyer of the Camden Theatre demanding 'We want Spike.' Their leader handed in a petition signed by over 1,030 listeners. It read, 'We, the undersigned, implore you, Spike Milligan, not to leave the country and forsake England for Australia, but to remain here and continue to write, produce and perform the Goon Show for ever and ever.' (Note that 'produce'!) Even before this, on February 11, a group of students from the Regent Street Polytechnic, near Broadcasting House, had besieged the BBC, waving banners reading 'Long Live Secombe' and 'Mind What You Do With Our Goons'.

In the end, it was decided to go ahead with a series of six shows. John Browell continued to produce, and Milligan was still writing on his own.

The first two shows are on the whole very good. 'A Christmas Carol' begins as a parody of the Dickens novel. ('Marley is dead. Marley is dead'—'No, I'm not'—BANG!—'*Yes you are*'.) It is knocking off time in the offices of Scrooge and Marley. ('Who's knocked off my sandwiches?') Eccles is sent to put the Christmas pudding, which contains £50,000 in gold threepenny bits, in the bank. Grytpype and Moriarty steal the pudding and escape on a mobile ladder. ('Can we hire this ladder?' — 'It doesn't go any higher, it's fully grown.') Seagoon pursues them in a conveniently nearby car, much to the surprise of Bluebottle. (''Ere — I was underneath that car, cleaning it! What a twinnick I look lyin' on my back in the middle of the road, one arm held up clutching a piece of oily rag. Supposin' a p'liceman had asked me what I was doing — I would say — Constabule — I cannot tell a lie — I'm breakin' the world's record for oily rag clutching.') The cast busk their way through the finale with a disorganized version of 'I'm Dreaming of a White Christmas'.

The second show, 'The Tale of Men's Shirts', involves a German plot to coat the tails of military soldier shirts with a chemical which, when the wearer sits down, will be exploded by the heat of his body. ('This way, the soldier will be neutralized' — 'It will be worse than that!') Meanwhile, everyone in England is writing his memoirs ('How I Saved De Gaulle And Told Mark Clark Where To Get Off'). Seagoon is sent into Germany to investigate the cause of the mysterious shirt explosions. He lands up in a prison which is full of British officers who have sworn to die rather than be captured. In the absence of any better ending, they are saved by the American Fifth Cavalry.

The writing was by now showing definite signs of strain. Apart from this, Milligan's mental processes were getting harder to follow. The remaining shows have very little form, although they contain some brilliant one-line gags. The overall result is very funny to a Goon fan, and incomprehensible to anyone else. The final show, 'The Last Smoking Seagoon', represents a noticeable drop in standards from even the beginning of this series. At the end, Greenslade says 'Yes, that was it, the last of them', and he was right.

Attempts were made to revive the shows, but they came to nothing. Milligan actually wrote six more scripts, but they were never performed. In his book *The Laughtermakers* David Nathan examines the last, unfinished, script in some detail. As he says, the spirits are more wild than high, and the laughter is chill. Milligan, interviewed for the book, admitted that 'there was one more throw of the dice to go, but I think that if we had thrown it we would have gone down and been forgotten. We got out while we were still on the top.' The shows ended at the right time, while they were still popular. The last rapid slide downhill was confined to the last few programmes, when the memory of the great shows of the 9th series was still fresh. There were attempts made from time to time to start the shows up again, but with Sellers spending much of his time filming in America, and Secombe and Milligan developing on their own, it proved impossible.

It is just as well. The long run of brilliant shows from the 5th series onwards stands up very well today, and the show is still amazingly popular, particularly considering that many of its fans are too young ever to have heard them in their original transmissions. Nothing could have done this popularity more damage than a succession of unsatisfactory shows. Also, the writing had caused Milligan a serious nervous breakdown and continuing depressions. Speaking later (in *Radio Times*), he said: 'It cost blood to put that show on for me. Sheer agony. It wrecked my first marriage and it wrecked my health. My nervous breakdown happened while I was on the show and I've been a neurotic ever since. So you can say I gave my sanity to that show.' If the shows had gone on they could only have damaged him still further. He had achieved the breakthrough in comedy that had been his aim when he started a decade earlier, and created a truly great comedy show.

Après Goon

The Goons, as a group, did not disappear entirely. Apart from the gramophone records of the show, there were a number of broadcasts on radio and television which showed that the spirit of Neddie Seagoon was still alive. The first of these were two series of fifteen-minute puppet films called 'The Telegoons', broadcast on BBC-TV in 1963 and 1964. Maurice Wiltshire re-worked the scripts of twenty-six original shows, and the three Goons recorded the sound track. Some of the puppets were quite successful in capturing the characters — Minnie, Henry, and Grytpype-Thynne in particular; but Seagoon, Bluebottle and Eccles were rather less effective. The whole thing inevitably lacked the pace and sparkle of the original shows, the final blow being the mistake of allowing pauses for laughs in the absence of an audience. For a time there were some people who, knowing no better, thought that the Telegoons *were* 'The Goon Show'.

Next came an appearance by the three Goons in a programme called 'Forces Gala Night', celebrating the 21st anniversary of the British Forces Broadcasting Service. They performed a shortened version of 'I Was Monty's Treble', with David Jacobs as the announcer in lieu of Greenslade who had died in 1961. (Jacobs had great difficulty in keeping a straight face.) The programme was broadcast on November 8, 1964 in the Light Programme; the last hour, which included the Goons, was also carried on the General Overseas Service.

In December 1964 Milligan and Secombe appeared together in 'The G.P.O. Show', which traced the history of the Post Office. Part of the script was a re-working of 'The History of Communications'. In 1966 and 1968 the Goons appeared on Independent Television performing from the original scripts, staged as if in a radio studio with no attempt to convert the shows for TV. (Details of all these broadcasts can be found in Appendix 4.)

Then, as part of the BBC's Jubilee celebrations in 1972, the cast, together with Geldray, Ellington, and members of the original orchestra, were assembled to perform a special 'Last Goon Show of All'. This is the show referred to by Milligan (in an interview with Margaret Howard) as being for the 50th anniversary of Lord Hill's legs — 'They've been together now for fifty years'. The recording session on April 30 was one of the last to take place in the Camden Theatre. A good deal of publicity was given to the event in the press, and the performance was also patronized by royalty — though not, to his own great disappointment, by their greatest royal fan, Prince Charles, whose naval duties prevented him from attending. The resultant show was certainly entertaining, but, as might be expected after a gap of twelve years, not up to the standard of the original shows. However, it did provide an interesting comparison with the rest of the BBC 'Light Entertainment' output of 1972, most of which was considerably inferior to any Goon Show. The recording was made in mono for Radio 4 (who don't believe in stereo: there seem to be times when they are not too sure about radio); Transcription Services took a separate feed from each microphone and made their own eight-track recording, which they re-mixed to produce the stereo version which has been issued by BBC Records; and BBC-TV broadcast a video recording of the proceedings the following Christmas.

There have been occasional rumours of another show, but at the time of writing nothing has come of them. One can always hope.

Various odd shows have been repeated by the BBC since the Goons disbanded. During 1974, Milligan became aware that there was a large number of Goon fans who were too young ever to have heard the programmes in the original transmissions. They persistently asked him when the shows would be repeated. He suggested to the BBC that they might like to run a series of repeats, offering to waive his fee. The BBC replied that they would be delighted to run a series, and paid a fee in the normal way. Ten shows were selected by John Browell from the Transcription Services' 'Pick of the Goons', and were broadcast starting on January 17, 1975 — the longest series of repeats for many years. The shows chosen were a varied bunch, but included several classics; and none of them had been repeated since 1960. Unfortunately, these versions are cut to 27 minutes. A number of listeners wrote complaining about the cuts; however as none of these shows exists intact — at any rate in broadcast-quality copies — it was a case of 27 minutes or nothing. It seems likely that there will be further series of repeats from time to time, as the interest in the Goons

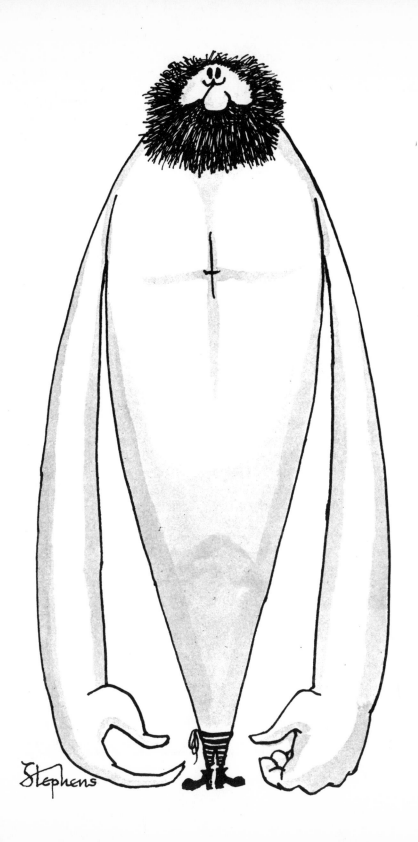

continues. The Goons can have had no idea what they were starting twenty-five years ago when the first edition of 'Crazy People' began:

ANNOUNCER What is the zaniest comedy show on the air today?
MILLIGAN Er — 'Today in Parliament'?
ANNOUNCER No, it's those Crazy People — THE GOONS.

The Method in the Madness

As Milligan has pointed out, 'The Goon Show' is thinking comedy. An often-quoted description of Goonism is 'bringing any situation to its illogical conclusion'. In fact, much of Goon humour depends on the *misuse* of logic. ('Major Bloodnok, Intelligence has established that the people attacking us are the enemy' — 'Gentlemen, do the enemy realise that you have this information?' — 'Oh no, we got 'em fooled, they think *we're* the enemy.') Another technique is to apply logical reasoning to an incorrect premise. There is a definite touch of paranoia about this example:

CRUN Get on baiting those elephant traps.
MIN I don't see the point of them, you know. We've never caught one.
CRUN That doesn't mean we must stop trying, Min of mine. Think of the dangers. Supposing you came down one morning for a greens-strainer and found an elephant in the larder, eh?
MIN Well, I've never seen an elephant in the larder.
CRUN That is because they're *hiding*, Min of mine.
MIN Where do elephants hide? Tell me that — where do elephants hide, buddy?
CRUN Well, I don't know, saxophone Min, but it's clear to me that they must hide *somewhere*. How else could they get away with it for so long?

('Queen Anne's Rain', 22-12-58; Milligan)

Another speciality of Milligan's is to leave out several steps of reasoning, and to arrive at a conclusion which leaves one feeling that he has a perfect right to be there, but wondering how on earth he managed it. (In prison — 'Bloodnok! How did you get in here?' — 'I have the OBE and attachment, also a parcel of steamed squids.')

However, the Goons are not limited by the existence of logic — they are quite capable of holding an argument without using it, simply going round in ever-decreasing circles until interrupted. Minnie and Henry are experts at that.

Often a remark will suddenly take a new twist of meaning and go off on its own ('The part of the mysterious stranger was played by Eccles. The rest of him was played by Rawicz and Landauer' — three different meanings in two sentences). From this technique it is of course only a small step to another favourite device — the pun, which Milligan absolutely revels in throughout the shows. (One ghost is arranging to meet another — 'How will I know you?' — 'I'll be wearing a reincarnation') Any excuse is taken for a pun — the worse, the better. ('Are you a spy?' — 'Yes' — 'Then why are you covered in mint?' — 'I'm a mint-spy!')

Milligan also became an expert in the fine art of capping jokes. Most writers can cap once; some twice; a few three times. Try this:

GRAMS	SHELL DROPPING
BLOODNOK	Duck!
GRAMS	HEN CLUCKING
SEAGOON	That's no duck, that's a chicken.
CHINSTRAP	By gad, sir, they're firing hens at us.
BLOODNOK	A *foul* trick.
CHINSTRAP	*Egg*-sactly.
MILLIGAN	We're being *shelled*.
SEAGOON	Stop cracking *yolks*!

('Shifting Sands', 24-1-57; Milligan and Stephens)

The Goons delighted in meaningless words and phrases. 'Yuckabakaka' is an early example. 'Ying-tong-iddle-i-po' became a popular catchphrase (but only after the cast had spent most of the 5th series working at it). Others are 'needle nardle noo' and 'hern hern', the latter being an encapsulation of the American language. Sometimes there is a touch of James Joyce about the proceedings: 'What agony igony ogony oogany mahogany!'

One of the rules of Goon humour is that there are no rules. Satire is mixed with fantasy, parody with caricature. Much of the style of all three artists arose out of their war service, reflecting a deep dislike of any form of regimentation. There is also a good deal of violence in the shows — characters are forever being blown up, dropped from great heights, drowned, or otherwise maltreated. However, no one ever comes to any real harm. Even in the most serious cases of Bluebottle-deading one is never left concerned for his eventual recovery. Eccles has the dynamite . . .

ECCLES	*(shouting)* I said, 'What comes after seven?'
BLUEBOTTLE	*(shouting, off)* I can't hear you!
ECCLES	*(shouting)* O.K. — I'll come over!
BLUEBOTTLE	*(shouting, off):* No, no! Do not bring that dreaded dynamite over here to me! I'll come over to *you*. *(Approaching)* Now then, what is it?

77

ECCLES	Well, I—
GRAMS	EXPLOSION
	(PAUSE)
ECCLES	Oooh! Bluebottle! Oooh . . . what's this custard on the wall?
BLUEBOTTLE	Don't you touch me, you rotten swine. Scrape me off and take me home.

('The Terrible Revenge of Fred Fu-Manchu', 6-12-55; Milligan)

Much of this aspect of Goonism arose out of the cast's great enthusiasm for Hollywood cartoons—Walt Disney, Tom and Jerry, and in particular, those directed by Chuck Jones, who created the 'Coyote and Road-runner' series for Warner Brothers. Also, it seems possible that the regular explosions in the show grew out of Milligan's own unpleasant experience in the war—perhaps in creating a world where explosions hurt no one, he made his own memories of the reality more bearable.

As has already been remarked, Peter Eton encouraged a lavatorial streak in the humour. In the face of official objections to this, a game developed of 'Let's put one over on the BBC'. The object of the exercise was to slip a dirty joke into the script in such a way that it was either not obvious, or else couldn't be objected to. One method was simply to quote the tag-lines of filthy jokes ('It's your turn in the barrel'). Another was the use of rhyming slang; a character called Hugh Jampton was introduced under Pat Dixon's nose—they told him it was the name of a friend who would be in the audience. (Hugh Jampton—Huge Hampton: Hampton Wick—work it out for yourself.) Frequently a joke that had not been removed from the recording before the first transmission caused a row the next day and was cut before the repeat. Transcription Services have tended to cut anything which is even faintly doubtful, unfortunately often ruining gags in the process. Of course, many of the remarks that caused trouble twenty years ago would pass unnoticed on the BBC today, but Transcription Services have to allow for the fact that some overseas audiences are not used to hearing this sort of humour on their radio stations.

An important part of the show is, of course, its use of sound effects. One of the most amazing aspects of Milligan's writing is his ability to describe, in cold blood, a complex effects sequence which, when it comes to life, sounds hilariously suitable, if inexplicable. As the series progressed, the noises became more and more complex. Milligan and the sound effects S.M.s spent hours pre-recording the exact effects required. Major Bloodnok's entrance became a regular cue for loud explosions, followed by remarks such as 'Whatever must the neighbours think?' The Radiophonics Workshop brought the full range of electronic techniques to bear on a recording of Bloodnok's stomach in action. He was also beset by the sound of dive-bombers ('Damn these mosquitoes') or, in 'World War One', an extremely noisy platoon of army socks.

It is a considerable tribute to the cast that they are never overshadowed by this profusion of strange sounds. The three main participants are, of course, all larger-than-life characters. The difference in their approach is interesting. Sellers started his professional life as an impressionist — and an exceptionally good one. His phonographic memory gives him an uncanny talent for mimicry — in fact his impression of Sir Winston Churchill is so good that he was asked to do the voice seriously for the sound-track of the film *The Man Who Never Was*. His control of the timbre of his voice is remarkable; each of his characters has a quite individual vocal tone (particularly the extraordinarily sexy female known as 'Cynthia' or 'Breathy Kensington Dear' — it really is difficult to believe that it isn't a genuine female voice). He identifies closely with each character as he plays it, switching from one to another with amazing facility (although he does occasionally get the wrong voice!). His approach is that of a professional actor — really he is a comic actor rather than a comedian. In his film career, he has assumed many different parts, moulding himself into the rôle as an actor, rather than having the film built round him as a character comedian, as, for instance, Frankie Howerd does. He has an excellent memory for lines, and the actor's trick of making a remark sound convincing even if he doesn't understand it — although he does occasionally sink a good gag by misreading it. He plays about a dozen major characters and a host of minor ones, investing each of them with a reality which is an essential factor in the show's success.

If Sellers is a professional actor, Milligan is a natural one. In some ways, Milligan's acting contribution to the show is more surprising, in view of his comparative lack of experience. His gallery of characters is smaller than Sellers's, but each of them is brilliantly observed and caricatured. His upper-class-twit voice is a piece of biting satire, and the major characters Minnie, Moriarty, and particularly Eccles, are no less living creations than Sellers's Crun, Grytpype-Thynne and Bloodnok. However, when working *outside* the Goon Shows he does not sink himself into different characters in the same way, but tends to remain identifiably himself. (Of course, Milligan as a writer-performer is a slightly different persona from Milligoon of the Goon Show.)

Secombe spends most of his time in the Goon Show as Neddie Seagoon, although he does have a number of minor parts — Old Uncle Oscar, Fred Bogg, Bluebottle's Mum, and so on. His knowledge of how to deliver his lines to their best advantage seems to be largely instinctive—although, like Milligan, his approach is rather different when separated from the other Goons. He also has a most infectious giggle which often escapes his attempts to suppress it during scenes between Bluebottle and Eccles, or Minnie and Crun. Unlike Sellers, who basically has a professional approach to his work and keeps his real personality well hidden, and Milligan, who underneath the clown is a serious and very melancholy person, Secombe is much the same bubbling personality off-stage. He has his serious side, but is a far less tense and more open personality than the others. He is also the proud possessor of a good singing voice, which has won him great popularity in the musical theatre—particularly in *Pickwick* and *The Plumber's Progress.*

These three diverse personalities contribute in their own ways to the dazzling display of juggling that makes 'The Goon Show' sound as if it has a cast of two dozen. Like those masters of another brand of comedy, Morecambe and Wise, they achieve the difficult task of making the show sound spontaneous when in fact a lot of careful work has gone into it. It is a popular myth that the shows contain a large proportion of ad-libs. In fact, any ad-libs made by the cast were often cut from the tape, and remarks that sound as though the speaker has just thought them up are almost always in the script. (Sellers occasionally remarks to the audience, when a line has earned a round of applause, 'It's all here, you know'.) Bloodnok's agonies ('Uoghgh! Aheheheheheh! Aggoiegh!') and Crun's ditherings ('Mnk . . . Mnk . . . ') are all scripted. It is a great tribute to Milligan's skill as a writer and the skills of all of them as performers that the show sounds so fresh and lively—a demonstration of the art that conceals art.

Music plays an important part in the show—perhaps because all three of the Goons are musicians in some degree—Secombe with his singing, Milligan with his trumpet, Sellers with his ukelele, drums, and atrocious piano playing. In the second series there are a number of sequences built round well-known tunes, often with words supplied by Jimmy Grafton. In some later shows, there are short songs performed by the characters. Bloodnok sings 'The Indigestion Waltz', Minnie sings 'I'm Going Out With a Mountain' as well as playing the saxophone—or nearly as well. Moriarty sings 'You Gotta Face Disaster With a Smile' (and he should know). Eccles sings a choral version of 'Good King Wenceslas' (with himself) and occasionally indulges in a tuneful solo on the bass drum. There are also several gags involving short excerpts from gramophone records—in particular 'The Harry Lime Theme' and a pre-electric recording of Jack Hylton's band playing 'Just Like a Thief' (HMV B.1588).

80

The orchestra also makes a major contribution to the proceedings. Wally Stott produced some excellent arrangements and link passages; these orchestrations and the first-class sound quality achieved by the studio managers make the band sound much larger than it is — usually twelve musicians plus the Ray Ellington Quartet as rhythm section. Special mention should be made of the master saxophonist E. O. Pogson, who had played with Jack Hylton, Jack Jackson *and* Jack Payne before the war; on a number of occasions he takes up his violin to provide a soulful and out-of-tune performance of 'Hearts and Flowers'. The Goons also involved the orchestra in the action from time to time — a tradition going back to 'ITMA' — and the players often put down their instruments and join Minnie in a chorus of 'Mor-ning!', or follow Milligan in shouting 'Thynneeeee!', which, as everybody knows, is the only cure for monkeys on the knee.

Special mention should also be made of the studio managers. In any technical medium — cinema, television, radio — the final result is a blend of the skills of many people; not only the actors and writers, the producer (or director) and the musicians, but also the technical staff who make possible the realisation of the other artists' ideas. Their contribution is no less important for being necessarily unobtrusive.

The shows, then, are a fusion of many factors — Milligan's writing, the cast's acting technique, the technical production, the music — all serving to provide the backcloth to the adventures of the strangest collection of characters ever to scramble their way into the radio sets of an unsuspecting public.

A Gallery of Idiots

The characters of 'The Goon Show' have been described as 'caricatures against a background of fantasy'. Unlike other radio shows, where the actors are playing the rôles in the story, 'The Goon Show' has actors who play characters; these characters then play the rôles in the plot, so that the action operates on three levels instead of two. In this way, characters frequently meet as if for the first time, because the plot demands it — but asides, made *in character*, make it clear that they 'really' know each other, and are indeed only acting. The Goons' creations also have a life of their own outside the radio studio. In *The Book of the Goons* there is a collection of letters and telegrams from the *characters* (rather than the artists) to each other, including several from elderly ladies vehemently denying that they are Major Bloodnok. Interviews with Milligan often contain observations from Eccles, who is evidently lurking just beneath the surface; Sellers frequently uses Bloodnok and other characters when he wishes to hide his own personality from reporters and interviewers; and Neddie

Seagoon can often be detected peering round the bubbling personality of Secombe. The listeners were often similarly affected. A generation of schoolboys grew up convinced that they were Bluebottle for at least some of the time—to the intense irritation of a generation of schoolmasters. Even today Henry Crun and Count Moriarty lurk unsuspected within many an apparently respectable citizen. The characters are so strongly drawn that they stand up to remarkably close scrutiny—when they can be persuaded to stand still for long enough.

A feature of the shows was the extraordinary names—even of the minor characters—Ernie Splutmuscle, Miss Fnutt, Scrongleshot Bowser, Councillor Major J. D. Windermere Ropesock, Q.C., and so on. Though a Bloodnok by any other name might smell as sweet, would he be as funny?

As the shows developed, major characters tended to pair up—Grytpype with Moriarty, Bluebottle with Eccles—Minnie and Henry had been paired since the early days. One character who firmly resisted this tendency was Major Bloodnok. Perhaps no one would have him. Bloodnok's inspiration was an Indian Army major whom Sellers had met during his service in India. Sellers had been entertaining himself by posing as an upper-class officer in the Officers' Mess—where he had no right to be. The major—though thoroughly in his cups—saw through the impersonation. Sellers beat a hasty retreat, but added another character to his mental file of voices for future use.

Bloodnok appears early in 'Crazy People'. At first he is more incompetent than anything else, but by the 3rd series he has developed most of his well-known characteristics. He is first and foremost a devout coward. However, he can be persuaded to take on almost any job—whether he knows how to do it or not—provided that there is the possibility of some cash in it. In the 4th and 5th series it is he who arranges the expeditions up Mount Everest or into the depths of the jungle. As time goes on he becomes more venal and even less reliable ('Me and the regimental funds took the wrong turning'). He is, in the end, willing to steal anything from anybody ('This pound note—what colour was it?'—'Green'—'It's mine! Mine was green!'). He is a martyr to sporadic dysentery and terminal indigestion, almost every appearance in the later series being heralded by cries of agony, loud explosions, and remarks such as 'No more curried eggs for me!' Despite these unendearing characteristics he seems to lead an active, not to say adventurous, love life—there is often a woman around somewhere ('Tell my ATS driver she can put the car away, I shall be needing her'). He is married, although we never meet Mrs. Bloodnok. ('My wife can't leave her bed'—'Why not?'—'I've sewn her in the mattress'—'Bloodnok, that's matricide!') He is never teamed up with any other major characters, but a small number of minor characters hover round him, over whom he still exerts some shreds of authority—Abdul, Singhiz Thingz, Gladys (played by Ray Ellington), and Sergeant Throat. Seagoon, it appears, was once his batman, and is always running across him, either coming to Bloodnok for advice or being discovered unconscious by him.

ORCHESTRA	BLOODNOK THEME
BLOODNOK	Oughgh! Aheheheheh! Oueoueghgh! Aggoieigh! Aheheheheh! Well, I can't sit here all day.
ABDUL	Sahib—Sahib—a Palladium-type-comic-type-gentleman has just collapsed in a heap outside.
BLOODNOK	I know—I tripped over that heap myself only this morning. I'll be glad when we're mechanized. Now lift up his wig and let's have a look at him.
SEAGOON	*(groans)*
BLOODNOK	Steady lad! Fan him with a thermometer, and put a copy of 'The Lancet' under his head.
SEAGOON	*(groans)*
ABDUL	Oh, goodness gracious, he is seriously unconscious, Major.
BLOODNOK	No wonder—I'll just lift that heavy wallet off him *(quick counting)* no wonder, there were forty pounds pressing on his chest. Now we'll just restore the circulation in his arms with the toad ointment.
SEAGOON	*(groans)*
BLOODNOK	Just put this pen in his hand and run it lightly over this cheque, there—
SEAGOON	Ah, oh, where am I?
BLOODNOK	In the red.
SEAGOON	Thank heavens—a British bank manager.
BLOODNOK	He's delirious. Hold him down while I force this brandy between my lips.
GRAMS	BUBBLING
BLOODNOK	Yes—you look much better now, lad.
SEAGOON	So do you.
BLOODNOK	Now, if you'll pardon me, I'll just stand in this hole facing north.
SEAGOON	Why?
BLOODNOK	It's all the rage, you know.
SEAGOON	Gad, it must be hell in there.
BLOODNOK	Further down, it *is*. Now lad, what brings you from the steaming hell of Finchley?
SEAGOON	I'm looking for the inventor of the telephone.

BLOODNOK	Ah, that's Crun, Henry Crun—so you're looking for that cool high-stepping fool, are you? Him and his sensual Caucasian knee-dancing—that's how he tempted poor Minnie away from me—Oh, Min!
SEAGOON	Come now, Major, Dennis, please—dry your tears on this marble statue of a handkerchief.
BLOODNOK	Thank you. Poor Min—abducted in the prime of her twilight. It's a long story—I remember it all started on the road to Mandalay—where the flying fishes play—and—oh!
SEAGOON	Yes yes yes yes—but that's your pigeon.
BLOODNOK	So it is! How did it get out? Abdul, take this pigeon away and bring me a clothes-brush.

('The Telephone', 13-12-56; Milligan and Stephens)

Bluebottle, one of the most popular characters in the show, was originally inspired by a large scoutmaster with a high-pitched voice, who was sent round to see Sellers by Bentine. The scoutmaster tried to persuade Sellers to participate at a boy's club concert. The high-pitched voice developed eventually into Bluebottle. Bluebottle's ancestor in the show was an idiot called Ernie Splutmuscle, who appeared as early as the second show in the first series. This character made occasional appearances, until in the third series he was cast for a small part in 'The Man Who Never Was' (show no. 20). Secombe strides across the ceiling of his club, hurling members to the floor. He bumps into Splutmuscle, who says 'No, do not hurl me to the floor'—'Are you a member?'—'No, I'm a Bluebottle'—'What's that you're reading?—'A fly-paper'. Four shows later, references to Everest are followed by the line: 'Greatest Mountain in the World', credited in the script to 'Peter (Bluebottle)'.

Bluebottle springs to life in the first show of the next series, 'The Dreaded Piano Clubber'. His appearance is marked by recorded applause, which he stops with 'Thank you, friends of the Bluebottle Fan Club'. By the ninth show of the series he is already reading his stage instructions. The voice at this stage is simply high-pitched rather than the strange falsetto effect which Sellers uses from early in the 5th series onwards.

Bluebottle is a self-styled cardboard-and-string hero. He is still at school, though always playing truant. His ideas of helping his nice captain, Seagoon, revolve round such reliable weapons as his cut-out cardboard Jet Morgan catapult. He is the one who is talked into doing the most dangerous work. He cannot be bribed—at least not with money—but will sell his soul for a quarter of dolly mixtures. He seems to have some sort of love-life in the background, to judge from the snippets of information he lets out about playground intrigues: 'I joined (the Foreign Legion) to forget a woman — Miriam Reene of 33 Croft Street, East Finchley. She turned me down for Dave Freeman — at playtime she said to me and Dave, "Who shows the most, gets me".' — 'You won?' — 'No; I only got a bit of string, and he got a fourpence and a saucer of water.'

His efforts to help his captain have the same result nearly every time — he falls foul of dynamite, and ends up 'deaded', much to his disgust. In fact he suffers a good deal of maltreatment, being kidnapped on many occasions by Ellington or Moriarty, and being threatened with fiendish tortures ('No, no, do not tie me to a stake' — 'Why not?' — 'I'm a vegetarian'). He is an unashamed solicitor of applause ('Enter Bluebottle, pauses for audience applause, not a sausage'); by the 6th series he is getting applause ('Ooh! Sosinges!') on nearly every occasion.

Bluebottle's best friend is Eccles, the 'original Goon'. He existed as a character before he had a name — in fact even before the Goon Shows started. His first appearance was as a stupid character, played by Milligan, appearing with Derek Roy in his series 'Hip Hip Hoo Roy'. Milligan was contributing a few gags to Jimmy Grafton's scripts for this series. Eccles is present in the early editions of 'Crazy People', but is not named until the seventh show, where one line is given to a character called Eccles, but played by Sellers! He is one of Captain Pureheart's team of assistants (Spalding, Carstairs and Eccles) building the Merseygoon Tunnel. The next week, in 'The Building of the Goonbird', Eccles appears in a similar situation, but this time the name is given to the correct character — Milligan's idiot voice. From then on he develops rapidly and is soon playing a major part in the series.

Eccles is a combination of village idiot (together with some of the village idiot's less desirable habits — 'Don't do that, Eccles, you'll get into trouble . . . you'll die') and Walt Disney's Goofy, with the latter's good-natured willingness to try anything — and make an incredible mess of it. At least Eccles has no illusions about himself — he *knows* he's an idiot, and never pretends otherwise. He never loses his temper, and never worries about anything. In 'Face Your Image' (BBC-1, 14-3-75), Jimmy Grafton said: 'Eccles, I think, is the nearest thing to, what you might say is Spike's own Id. A very simple, uncomplicated character, who doesn't want to be burdened with the responsibility of thinking, and just wants to be happy and enjoy himself. And I think that, fundamentally, is Spike. I've always told him that I think Eccles is the true Milligan, and the rest is just a cover.' Milligan's reaction: 'I'm afraid he's right, yes, yes. That's it, man, you know, I don't want to think about earning money, I just want to be an idiot. Oh, I'd stand up to my neck in a bucket of custard, and enjoy it, you know.' Unlike Milligan, however, Eccles never has to cope with income tax, or deadlines—being an idiot absolves him from any form of responsibility. Whereas Bluebottle is usually waiting in the wings for a summons ('I heard you call, my Capatain!'), Eccles turns up unasked ('Here, here, what's going on 'ere?'—'Nothing'—'Oh, I'll clear off then').

It was inevitable that Bluebottle and Eccles should come together. In the 5th series, they tend to appear separately, meeting occasionally and asking each other questions like 'What school do you go to?' Gradually their friendship blooms, and by the 7th series the plots regularly stop completely to let them have one of their hilarious discussions, like this one, which is taken very slowly.

BLUEBOTTLE	What time is it, Eccles?
ECCLES	Um, just a minute, I got it written down here on a piece of paper. A nice man wrote the time down for me this morning.
BLUEBOTTLE	Euh! Then why do you carry it around with you, Eccles?
ECCLES	Well, um, if anyone asks me the time, I can show it to them.
BLUEBOTTLE	Wait a minute, Eccles my good man —
ECCLES	What is it, fellow?
BLUEBOTTLE	It's writted on this bit of paper — what is eight o'clock, is writted.
ECCLES	I know that, my good fellow—that's right, when I asked the fellow to write it down it was eight o'clock.
BLUEBOTTLE	Well, then, supposing when somebody asks you the time it *isn't* eight o'clock?
ECCLES	Well, then I don't show it to them.
BLUEBOTTLE	Well, how do you know when it's eight o'clock?
ECCLES	I got it written down on a piece of paper.
BLUEBOTTLE	I wish I could afford a piece of paper with the time writted on. Here, Eccles—let me hold that piece of paper to my ear, would you? . . . Here—this piece of paper ain't going!
ECCLES	What? I've been sold a forgery!
BLUEBOTTLE	No wonder it stopped at eight o'clock. You should get one of them things my grand-dad's got. His firm give it to him when he re-tired. It's one of them things what it is that wakes you up at eight o'clock, boils the kettule, and pours a cup of tea.
ECCLES	Oh, yeah — what's it called . . .
BLUEBOTTLE	My Grandma.

ECCLES   Ah. Here — wait a minute — how does *she* know when it's
             eight o'clock?
BLUEBOTTLE   She's got it written down on a piece of paper.

('The Mysterious Punch-up-the-Conker', 7-2-57; Milligan and
     Stephens)

Henry Albert Sebastopol Queen Victoria Crun (Sellers) is an elderly,
slow, rather dim inventor. He is a craftsman of the old school, which is
why he is always so concerned about the shortage of raw materials
('You can't get the wood, you know'). Over the years he invents and
builds many strange things, to some extent taking over from that other
inventor, Osric Pureheart. His interest in things mechanical leads him
into some odd places — notably the interiors of rosewood pianos and
grandfather clocks ('Stop dancing the modern rumba, buddy' — 'I'm
not dancing the modern rumba, Min! I've got the pendulum stuck
down my trousers!'). He is often approached by Seagoon when special
equipment is required for some unlikely undertaking; he is most
helpful in intention, but tends to meander off the subject. He is not so
much stupid as very slow, and very forgetful — often forgetting what
was said to him only a few seconds ago.
    Crun lives with Minnie Bannister (Milligan), once the toast of the
Indian Army ('The Darling of Roper's Light Horse — also of his heavy
one') and now an elderly lady specializing in modern rhythm-type
saxophone playing and living in constant fear (hope?) of being
attacked ('We'll all be murdered in our beds'). She first appears rather
later than Henry — in the tenth of the 2nd series, Pureheart gets a
telephone call from his 'Auntie Bannister'. In the eighteenth show,
Minnie and Henry appear together for the first time — Henry
introduces her as his wife. (That should settle any doubts arising in the
later series.) In the first show of the 4th series Minnie claims to be
Henry's auntie — a likely story. It emerges much later that she is also
Bluebottle's auntie — and in 'The Childe Harolde Rewarde' they both
masquerade as the parents of Neddie Seagoon, insisting that he is a
baby ('Dib, dib, dib'). Many of Minnie's appearances are in the
distance, enquiring what Henry is up to; and as both of them are slow-
witted and deaf, it is hardly surprising that any discussion between
them tends to turn into an argument. They have a total mental block
on the subject of doors, particularly locked doors. Whenever they
meet this situation the result is absolute chaos.

FX   DISTANT KNOCKING
CRUN   *(snoring)* Mnk — dear, dear, dear — why must people call in
         the middle of the night, why can't they come at a
         reasonable — Min?

MIN	What, what, what — yes, buddy?
CRUN	There's somebody knocking, Min.
MIN	Yes, Henry, yes — there's somebody knocking.
CRUN	One of us will have to answer the door, Min.
MIN	Oh dear — you answer it, Henry — I can't find my boot in the dark.
CRUN	Well then — turn on the light, Min.
MIN	I *can't* , Henry.
CRUN	Why not?
MIN	When it's dark I can't find the light. (PAUSE)
CRUN	I've just had a clever idea, Minnie.
MIN	Have you, Henry?
CRUN	Yes, Min dear, it is a very *clever* idea.
MIN	Ohhhhhh. How did you come to think of it, Henry?
CRUN	You know, it came to me when I was thinking about . . . thinking . . . er . . . Min?
MIN	Yes, Henry?
CRUN	I've forgotten what it was I was thinking about when I got the idea.
MIN	Oh — never mind, Henry — what was the idea?
CRUN	I've forgotten, Min.
MIN	Oh. (PAUSE)
CRUN	Min?
MIN	Yes, Henry?
CRUN	He's stopped knocking.
MIN	Perhaps he's gone away, buddy.
CRUN	Oh dear, what a pity.
MIN	Why, Henry?
CRUN	I've just remembered the clever idea.
MIN	What was it, Henry?
CRUN	Well, we should throw the key out of the window, Min.
MIN	Oh! That *was* a clever idea, Henry.
CRUN	Yes, it was, wasn't it. (PAUSE)
MIN	Henry? — Supposing he comes back?
CRUN	Well, he won't be able to get in, Min. You can't get in without the key, you know, you must have the key to get in with.
MIN	But he hasnt't *got* the key, Henry.
CRUN	What key, Min?
MIN	The *key* to the *door.*
CRUN	Well, then he won't be able to get in.

88

MIN	No, Henry, I know that.
CRUN	He must have the key, Min, otherwise he can't get through the door.
MIN	I know—but you've got the key, Henry.
CRUN	Yes, then he can't get in. He must have the key, you know, you can't get in without keys. . . .
MIN	Yes—oh dear—why don't you throw the key out of the window, Henry?
CRUN	Oh—that's an idea, isn't it!
MIN	It's a clever idea.
CRUN	Yes—how did you ever think of such a clever idea? (PAUSE)
MIN	What idea, Henry?
CRUN	The idea that . . . what . . . what *was* the idea, Min?
MIN	*(fed up)* I don't know, I've no idea, Henry.
CRUN	But you said you had one, Min.
MIN	*(getting irritated)* Had one *what*?
CRUN	*(annoyed)* That's what I'm asking you.
MIN	What are you asking me about?
CRUN	You stupid old—I was asking you. . . .
MIN	Don't you start shouting at me again—OOOoooooOOOh! (once round the room does me good, you know)—oh dear—
FX	KNOCKING
CRUN	He's knocking again, Min.
MIN	I know, Henry, I know.
CRUN	One of us will have to answer the door, Min.
MIN	You answer it, Henry, I can't find my boot in the dark.
SEAGOON	*(off)* Hey—if you don't want to come down, throw me the key and I'll let myself in.
MIN	Throw him the key, Henry.
CRUN	That's a very clever idea, Min.

('The Great Tuscan Salami Scandal', 21-2-56; Milligan)

Minnie is something of a secret tippler, and is frequently somewhat the worse for alcohol or whoopee pills, much to Henry's irritation ('Stop it, you drunken old fool'). There seems in the past to have been a romantic liaison with Bloodnok, for any meeting between them in the later series is characterized by feminine flutters from Minnie, and romantic protestations from Bloodnok ('I'm taking you away from the squalor that you live in, to the squalor that *I* live in'). Henry takes a dim view of all this, but since Sellers is playing Bloodnok at the time, there is little Henry can do about it.

Unlike many comedy characters, the Goons' creations have sufficient life of their own to develop in their own way, often in directions which one suspects Milligan had never intended. The most interesting case of this character development is that of the dual villains Moriarty and Grytpype-Thynne. Grytpype does not get his name until the beginning of the 5th series, but appears as early as the end of the 2nd series in the form of the suave-voiced character not named in the dialogue, but identified in the script as 'Sanders'. He is closely modelled on the late George Sanders, although sometimes he seems to develop a touch of the Valentine Dyalls. He plays various minor rôles until starting to develop into a major character in the latter half of the 4th series. At the very beginning of the 5th series he springs into full life as Lance-Brigadier Hercules Grytpype-Thynne, sending Seagoon on a secret mission. In 'The Dreaded Batter-Pudding Hurler' he is a police inspector. This high moral tone does not last long, however, due to the bad influence of a certain fiendish criminal and French schemer, Count Jim Moriarty.

Moriarty appears in the second show of the 3rd series, at the far end of a telephone. The script says: 'Spike (*slightly French*)'. At this stage Moriarty is a Conan-Doyle-type master criminal, spreading a net of international intrigue from his hide-out in France. With Milligan's nervous breakdown, Sellers took over the rôle for the remainder of the series (even after Milligan's return). However, with the beginning of the 4th series, Moriarty is once again played by Milligan, taking full Gallic part in the action, and making noises like 'Sapristi Bompetts!' All during the 4th series he is to be found at the root of the complicated crimes in which Seagoon finds himself involved. Moriarty is efficient, well-organized, and fully self-controlled; his downfall is yet to come.

In the same show in which Grytpype is an inspector of police, Moriarty of course *is* the Dreaded Batter-Pudding Hurler. Two shows later, in 'The Affair of the Lone Banana', Moriarty appears under Grytpype's command — the first time they work together. A further two shows later, in 'Lurgi Strikes Britain', they appear for the first time acting together in a plot against Seagoon — the beginning of a long partnership of crime. Interestingly, this coincides with the beginning of Eric Sykes's co-authorship of the shows.

Moriarty is efficient for some time, but the first symptom of his gradual decline can be heard in his greed: 'Ah, the money, the moolah, the grisbee, ah — lovely money, moneyyyyy.' Then the expression 'Owww', pronounced 'Owww', rears its head. This gradually becomes an obsession with him, not helped by the release in December 1956 of his record 'You Gotta Go Owww!'. At first Grytpype is able to keep him rationed to a few 'Owws' per programme, but gradually the rot sets in. Even a visit to the London of Samuel Pepys is unable to effect a cure.

SEAGOON   *(Pepys)* Now, with whom can I make gossip this chilly morn? I see nobody, though, and nobody sees me — what a coincidence, Egad, espon, to be sure, hern hern, hi diddle dee, needle nardle noo, splin splan splon, ying tong iddle-i po, and remember — you've got to go 'Owww!'

GRYTPYPE   How very interesting that was.

SEAGOON   I'm sorry — I didn't see you standing in that coffee-pot.

GRYTPYPE   I know — we had the lid down.

SEAGOON   We? Where's your friend?

GRYTPYPE   He's up the spout.

MORIARTY   Owwww. You gotta go 'Owwwwwwww.'

SEAGOON   Ye spon — he's just been 'Owwwwwwww!'

GRYTPYPE   Yes, it's all the rage. Now, have these two seats been taken?

SEAGOON   No, they're still here! *(Laughs hysterically)* Ahem!

GRYTPYPE   A Charlie.

SEAGOON   What, what, whatwhatwhatwhatwhatwhatwhatwhat?

GRYTPYPE   I was only nearly saying that the other day. This is my friend, Count Jim 'Thighs' —

MORIARTY   Owwwww.

GRYTPYPE   — Moriarty, Minister without Underpants to the Principality of Monte Carlo.

SEAGOON   A German diplomat is always welcome in England.

MORIARTY   What? Sapristi nuckoes — hairy insult! You insult me, a Frenchman — we must fight a duel.

FX   TWO SHOTS

MORIARTY   Honour is satisfied!

SEAGOON   And so am I!

ORCHESTRA   THIN CHORD, SNAP CYMBAL.

GRYTPYPE   Sir, you will excuse this steaming Gaul — he's given to short temper as he has no lodgings for the night.

SEAGOON   So! I can't see a French Count sleeping in the street.

MORIARTY   Of course not, I've got up now. Owwww, owwwww.

GRYTPYPE   *(annoyed)* He's just been 'Owww' again!

SEAGOON   I should like to accommodate you for the night, but —

MORIARTY   We accept!

GRYTPYPE   I second that. Moriarty, go and pack the jam-tins.

SEAGOON   *(narration)* Did return home with the two gentlemen. Did not sport with Mrs. FitzSimmonds owing to the cold weather and the presence of the French Count and his manager, who occupied my second-best bed.

GRYTPYPE	You heard that nice gentleman, Moriarty, put on your second-best pyjamas.
MORIARTY	Owwww, owwwww.
GRYTPYPE	There he goes again—he never thinks of anything else these days. By the way, Moriarty—did you notice the brass name-plate on our host's door?
MORIARTY	Yes, I've got it here.
GRYTPYPE	You clever little vandal, you. You see what it says—Samuel Pepys, Secretary to the Navy. We couldn't have picked a better Charlie for our plan.
MORIARTY	Owwww, owwwww, sapristi nadgers, if it works, we'll get rich beyond the dreams of Olwen—owww, the money, the moolah, the grisbee—owwwww, owwwww, owwwwwwwww, ow!
GRYTPYPE	He's going to have one of his turns again.

('The Flea', 20-12-56; Milligan and Stephens)

Worse is to come. In the 8th series shows, Moriarty is clamouring for *food*, lovely food, never mind money. He is by now a sad case, cringing, owwwing, and unable to say more than about a sentence at a time coherently. An interesting difficulty arises in the 'Vintage Goons' series, because the modern cringing Moriarty ('who has played the male lead in over fifty postcards') is having to read lines originally intended for the old efficient Moriarty. The result is a little odd.

What is at first not so obvious is that he drags Grytpype-Thynne down with him. In the 5th series they stay in hotels on the Riviera—by the 8th they are to be found living in dustbins, down sewers, or up trees. This one-time Lance-Brigadier is sadly degraded. ('Pass me the finger-bowl, Moriarty—you greedy swine!—you've eaten the last finger!') They are to sink even lower. ('Keep still—do you want us both out of this suit?') By the 9th series Moriarty's downfall is complete ('Now, which of all these fish-bones is you?').

Milligan's biographical notes in the first book of Goon Show scripts make it clear that Grytpype is a practising homosexual. This is not immediately evident from listening to the shows, because Grytpype succeeds in keeping the matter under wraps—as indeed he would have to, homosexuality being at that time a criminal offence, even between consenting adults in dustbins. There are very occasional slight hints in the tone of voice he employs; and Milligan's exposé of the matter throws into sharper relief this exchange (from 'The Telephone').

GRYTPYPE	You'll pardon the mess, we can't help it really, we're bachelors.
SEAGOON	Why don't you get married?

GRYTPYPE   *I* would, but Moriarty doesn't love me.

The gradual decline of the two characters is particularly fascinating as it is too slow to have been the result of a deliberate decision, and indeed only really becomes clear in retrospect. There are cases of deliberate changes being made to a character—for example, Crun's voice drops in pitch between the end of the 5th series and the beginning of the 6th, presumably to differentiate him more clearly from Minnie. But in the case of Grytpype and Moriarty, the natural development of the characters leads to this slow but devastating decline to the depths of degradation. Perhaps this reflects a jaundiced view of humanity on Milligan's part; or perhaps the characters were simply imposing their own will on their creator.

Apart from these main characters, there is a large collection of minor rôles; the most important of these is Willium. This elderly, despairing Cockney never quite becomes a major character although he turns up in many shows from the 4th series on. Identifying himself on several occasions as 'Sewer Man Sam', and meandering dolefully through the shows calling everyone 'Mate', he was originally based on a Kenneth Connor character in 'Ray's a Laugh'. Sellers developed the character into the asthmatic pessimistic down-and-out, perpetually assuming an authority he does not have (''Ere, you two men, what you doin' there?'). He divides his time between the labour exchange ('Any fear of *work* today?') and the police force, often appearing as a constable on the beat. Milligan tells us that Willium was last seen working as a doorman at the BBC's studios at Aeolian Hall in Bond Street; many of the earlier shows were recorded there, and it also housed the offices of the Variety Department.

A character who pops up in most of the shows from the 6th series onwards is Jim Spriggs, played by Milligan. Spriggs is often a minor official, such as a court usher ('The court will rise—and then come down again'). He habitually addresses everybody as 'Jim' pronounced 'Jeem', usually in the form of his catchphrase,

Hello Jim!

Though he does not usually involve himself too closely in the plot, he is capable of a pointed retort when necessary ('What does *that* mean?'—'It means you're ignorant, Jim').

Milligan also plays another member of the Spriggs family—Adolphus Spriggs, a wandering singer who sometimes masquerades under the name of Jim Pills. He insinuates himself into the action, often trying to burst forth into a rendering of his favourite ballad, 'I'm Only a Strolling Vagabond', much to the irritation of those around him. He usually gets shot.

Two very popular characters who appear comparatively late are the Indian gentlemen, Singhiz Lalkaka and Babu Banerjee ('Babu' means 'clerk'). They begin their lives as a single voice — Bloodnok's servant Singhiz Thingz (Abdul is a very close relative). In 'The Red Fort' (seventh of the 8th series), Lalkaka and *Lakajee*, assisted by Singhiz (played for once by Secombe) have terrible trouble with a key they are making to fit a stolen door. The names are really too similar, as the cast have a certain amount of difficulty with them. They appear later in the series, in 'The String Robberies', as Lalkaka and Banerjee. Their mutterings at each other in heavily curry-flavoured English soon became a highly popular feature of the show; Transcription Services identify *every* programme they appear in with references in the publicity material to 'our old friends Lalkaka and Banerjee', but this is more by way of a warning to broadcasters who feel that their audience might be upset by them. There is also a rumour that the two mutter doubtful phrases at each other in Hindustani.

In a sketch in the first series Milligan had propounded the theory that a catchphrase was simply a meaningless remark repeated until the audience was brainwashed into laughing at it. He illustrated this with a character opening a door, shouting 'More Coal!', and exiting again. It was demonstrated that on the first hearing, this was followed by dead silence; on the thousandth it was greeted by rapturous (pre-recorded) applause. In the character of Little Jim he seems to have set out to demonstrate the truth of this observation. Little Jim is mentioned long before he actually appears — in 'The House of Teeth', (6th series), Bluebottle, in distress once again, calls upon Little Jim for help. He gets no answer, which is hardly surprising, as Little Jim is in Africa. In 'The Rent Collectors' (sixteenth of the 7th series), Secombe falls into the river. Sellers prepares the way for Milligan by saying: 'Oh dear, children — look what has happened to poor Uncle Harry.' Milligan, as a 'very dull young child', answers — 'He's fallen in the wa-ter!' This is repeated a couple of times during the show. (In 'Wings over Dagenham', recorded earlier on the same evening, Milligan says, quite irrelevantly, and more to himself than anyone else, 'He fell in the wa-ter'; only Secombe, who of course knows what is coming in the next show, reacts.) Two weeks later, in 'The Moon Show', Bluebottle is asked for an explanation of why he has appeared wearing only his pyjama top. It seems that Little Jim has borrowed Bluebottle's pyjama trousers in order to give an imitation of an elephant — and then slipped into the bath. 'Tell them what happened, Little Jim' — 'I fell in the wa-ter!' (Milligan was still experimenting with his new catchphrase). After that, Little Jim confines himself to pointing out when other people have fallen in the wa-ter—a frequent occurrence. He occasionally holds baby-language conversations with Bluebottle and Eccles—a successor to Harry Hemsley's unintelligible baby Horace. By the end of the next series, Little Jim's catchphrase is always greeted with a huge round of applause. Milligan has proved his point.

There are far too many minor characters to mention them all. Milligan produces an extraordinary sort of controlled belch, close to the microphone; this character is known as 'Throat', or sometimes 'Miss Throat'. Sellers uses a very 'camp' voice for Flowerdew, who appears in many of the early shows, but from the 5th series onwards makes only brief appearances ('Oooh, I could *spit!*'), hardly ever being referred to by name. Sellers's Jewish impresario, Lew (who never quite makes the Grade), sometimes referred to in the script as 'Cash', also appears as Judge Schnorrer, and in various unlikely places including the German Army ('What am I doin' in *this* army, my life?'). Lew is the promoter behind the successful announcers Greenslade and Eccles in 'The Greenslade Story' ('Eccles, Schmeccles, my lovely boy . . . ') and also controls the purse strings when Seagoon needs to be ransomed in 'Ye Bandit of Sherwood Forest' ('I'll send a geezer on his way with the gelt to get you out of schtuck'). Under the name of Leslie Grisbeck he takes over the explanation of Crun's brilliant idea in 'The Man Who Never Was' when Henry gets too muddled to continue ('Now look, listen, I'm his agent, let me talk for 'im. I'll talk for 'im, he's a bit schtumm, er, so 'e can't talk a bit').

Milligan's continuing fascination with the Scottish poet and tragedian William McGonagall, who wrote some of the most lame-footed verse imaginable, first shows itself in 'The Saga of HMS Aldgate' (fourth of the 3rd series), the first of many stories to be introduced by a few succinct lines of verse read by William J. MacGoonigal—played sometimes by Milligan, sometimes by Sellers. His verse adds a definite air of culture to the shows he appears in:

"*Twas in the year 1884 and in the month of June,
That Major Bloodnok and his gallant men were besieged
    in Khartoum.
Besieged by the Mahdi's savage men, they formed a thin
    red line;
But the Mahdi did not care at all, for he was Mahdi fine.*'

Last, but not least (particularly as regards girth) comes the central character, Neddie Seagoon, around whom all these other oddities revolve. Played by Secombe in his own voice (but more so) this patriotic, gullible, enthusiastic incompetent, always down on his luck (and everyone else's), is the mainstay of most of the plots. An overweight midget, suffering from duck's disease (short legs), it is he who is conned into exporting snow to the Sudan, climbing Everest from the inside, or insuring the English Channel against catching fire. Like Tommy Handley in 'ITMA', Neddie stays 'on-stage' for much of the show, while the other characters come on in ones or twos to provide the background to his adventures. (The difference from 'ITMA' is that once Handley had arrived, he stayed on-mic for the rest of the show. Seagoon often retires into the background, either to allow a plot against him to brew, or to allow Bluebottle and Eccles or Minnie and Henry their non-plot sequences. Whereas 'ITMA' was specifically built round Handley, in 'The Goon Show' none of the artists is starred above the others.)

Secombe's performance as Neddie is a masterpiece of over-acting; shouting, panicking, addressing the audience (through a *megaphone*, yet) and bursting into ear-splitting song at the least provocation. Grytpype has his measure ('A Charlie!'), and can generally dupe him with ease, luring him into complex plots designed to rebound on Seagoon and keep Grytpype and Moriarty in the monies for the remainder of their lives. Seagoon will take any course of action, provided that he can be persuaded that it is a matter of honour. ('You know, that's the sort of thing I'd do. Honori Tempus and Gratis, Up The School, Last Man In and Ten Runs To Get (*sings*) Boots, Boots, Boots, Boots, Tramping Over Africa, *There's No Discharge IN THE WAR !!!!*' — 'You silly twisted boy, you.') These plots usually misfire, since Seagoon is too stupid to fool even himself. Eccles and Bluebottle still look up to him as their leader, but Bloodnok loses no opportunity to remove Seagoon's wallet and money-belt; while Minnie and Henry are never too sure who he is anyway.

Since it is the other characters one tends to think of first when remembering the show, it might be imagined that Seagoon was the most dispensable character; however, when Secombe was unable to attend and his place was taken by Dick Emery or Kenneth Connor, the difference was marked. Emery, although an experienced and excellent comedian in his own right, is unable to adapt to the pace of the show, and sounds completely out of his depth ('Spon', first of the 8th series). Although Connor manages better by playing his part at a larger pitch, he still does not fit into the show at all well ('The £50 Cure', seventeenth of the 9th series). Secombe, although he plays only a handful of characters, and all those apart from Seagoon are very minor ones, fulfils an important function in holding the show together. His central rôle acts as the pivot around which the gallery of grotesques can act out Milligan's fantasies.

96

Also Taking Part Were . . .

'This is the BBC Home Service—*and I'm getting fed up saying it!*'
Unlike most other comedy shows, the Goons were rarely content to
allow their announcer to stick to his official job. Andrew Timothy had
found himself involved in the plot of the Goons' sketches even as early
as the first series. Greenslade was rapidly drawn into the programme
in the same way; in the 5th series, he *is* the Phantom Head Shaver, and
he is the one who finally gets the Spanish Suitcase full of stolen money.
Several programmes are elevated by the appearance of John Snagge,
who had been a behind-the-scenes supporter of the Goons since their
early days. Andrew Timothy also makes a brief reappearance, in 'The
Scarlet Capsule', with pre-recorded announcements originally
intended for Snagge ('I would like it known that though I read this
stuff, I don't write it').

The musicians contribute more than melody to the show.
Geldray, possibly the world's worst actor, takes a few odd lines; and
Ray Ellington makes frequent appearances as Gladys, Chief Ellinga,
and Major Bloodnok's old enemy, the Red Bladder. His appearance is
usually enough to send Bloodnok scurrying for cover. He also provides
the basis for a number of 'colour' jokes, most of which have had to be
removed from the Transcription Services versions. (For example, he is
referred to on several occasions as 'Black Rod'.) George Chisholm
occasionally steps out of the orchestra to speak a few lines in a sporran
language. The Goons also established a tradition of guest artists
during Milligan's long absence in the 3rd series. Their appearances
are charted in the 'Goonography'.

The Goons—In a Nutshell

Attempts to transfer Goon humour to other media have met with
varying degrees of success. The artists made a few appearances in
second feature films in the early 1950s (see Appendix 7), but the need
to assemble the films in short takes and the absence of an audience
prevented the Goon style of humour from taking flight. The most
successful of the Goon appearances was *The Case of the Mukkinese
Battle Horn*, a short film made in 1956 under extreme difficulties,
without Secombe, who was unable to participate, and with Milligan
making the script up as he went along. This film turned up in 1975 as
the supporting programme to *Monty Python and the Holy Grail*, and
stood up extremely well.

In 1956 Sellers and Milligan appeared in three series on
ITV—'Idiot Weekly Price 2d', 'A Show Called Fred', and 'Son of Fred'
(see Appendix 4). The shows contained some good moments, but
television—which was at that time still largely 'live'—was not really

able to cope with Milligan's approach. It was not until his series 'Q5' in 1969 that his sort of humour really worked on the small screen. 'Q5' itself provided some of the inspiration for the TV show which, at its best, might be considered a worthy successor to the Goons — 'Monty Python's Flying Circus'.

Perhaps the greatest compliment to 'The Goon Show' is that, sixteen years after it ended, it is still not only popular, but the shows sound fresh and extremely funny. They also stand up well to repetition — a severe test for any form of comedy. Of all the BBC's comedy series only 'ITMA' was ever more popular, and 'ITMA' never stirred up the controversy that 'The Goon Show' created before it even got on the air. This perhaps is the secret of the Goons' lasting success. Whereas 'ITMA' was fairly gentle — even affectionate — in its lampooning of authority (there was, after all, a war on for half the time 'ITMA' was on the air), 'The Goon Show' was frequently in trouble for its lack of respect for the Establishment — or indeed for anybody. Whereas 'ITMA' was liked by almost everybody at the time, opinion was always sharply divided as to 'The Goon Show'. Interestingly, practically nobody was indifferent to the Goons; people were either enthusiastic or hated the whole thing.

Rooted firmly in the nonsense of Lewis Carroll, the satire of Aristophanes, the anarchy of the Marx Brothers, the violence of the Hollywood cartoon, and the broad comedy of the English Music Halls, the Goons brought to the air a use of the techniques of sound broadcasting rarely achieved by any radio organization. The freedom of imagination which only radio can provide, coupled with painstaking use of sound effects to produce results highly organized to seem effortless, produced what can fairly be described as the greatest comedy series ever broadcast. Of all the other shows, only 'ITMA' approaches 'The Goon Show' in greatness, because of its high polish, its tremendous speed (it is still the fastest-paced show, and that without benefit of pre-recording or editing) and creation of its own individual world. To this the Goons added an expansion of the use of the medium made possible by advances in the technical side, and a greater variation of approach than 'ITMA'.

Their influence is still felt. On June 9, 1975 the proceedings of the House of Commons were broadcast for the first time. The *Daily Mirror* complained the next day that the microphones picked up the shouting, cheering and protests too loudly, making Question Time sound more like a Goon Show than MPs at work. The *Mirror* went on to say that the Goon Show's representation of the House of Commons sounded more like the real thing than the real thing did.

The Goon Show lives! Vivat Milligna!

SOURCES OF QUOTATIONS IN THE TEXT

Quotations, identified by their page numbers and first line, are listed in order of appearance in the text, with the show they appear in and its series/number reference. Quotations which have been identified in the text are ignored, as are catchphrases. There are a few quotations which it has not been possible to trace.

p.42   'Please report your exact position' — 'Crazy People', programme 5.

p.55   'See you later, Alligator' — 'Insurance, the White Man's Burden' (7/21)

p.76   'Major Bloodnok, Intelligence has established . . . ' — 'The Battle of Spion Kop' (9/9)
'Bloodnok! How did you get in here?' — 'Robin's Post' (10/4)
'The part of the mysterious stranger . . . ' — 'The Mystery of the Fake Neddie Seagoons' (7/9)

p.77   'Are you a spy?' — 'The Jet-Propelled Guided NAAFI' (6/19)
'What agony igony ogany oogany mahogany' — 'The Battle of Spion Kop' (9/9)

p.78   'Whatever must the neighbours think?' — 'Queen Anne's Rain' (9/8)

p.80   'The Indigestion Waltz' — 'The Policy' (8/9)
'I'm Going Out With a Mountain' — 'The White Neddie Trade' (8/19)
'You Gotta Face Disaster With a Smile' — 'The Burning Embassy' (8/3)
'Good King Wenceslas' — 'The String Robberies' (8/16) *and* 'Ned's Atomic Dustbin' (9/10)

p.82   'Me and the regimental funds . . . ' — 'The House of Teeth' (6/20)
'This pound note . . . ' — 'The Lost Emperor' (6/3)
'No more curried eggs for me!' — 'Dishonoured — Again' (9/13)
'Tell my ATS driver . . . ' — 'Ten Snowballs that Shook the World' (8/20)
'My wife can't leave her bed' — 'Shangri-La Again' (6/8)

p.85   'I joined to forget a woman . . . ' — 'The Gold Plate Robbery' (9/16)
'No, no, do not tie me to a stake' — 'Ye Bandit of Sherwood Forest' (5/14)
'Don't do that, Eccles . . . ' — 'The Gold Plate Robbery' (9/16)

p.86   'Here, here, what's going on 'ere?' — various shows, e.g. 'Tiddleywinks' (8/24)
'What school do you go to?' — 'The Dreaded Batter-Pudding Hurler' (5/3)

p.87   'Stop dancing the modern rumba, buddy' — 'The Plasticine Man' (8/13)
'The Darling of Roper's Light Horse . . . ' — 'The Terrible Revenge of Fred Fu-Manchu' (6/12)

p.89   'Stop it, you drunken old fool!' — 'The Moriarty Murder Mystery' (8/17)
'I'm taking you away from the squalor . . . ' — 'The Telephone' (7/11)

p.92   'who has played the male lead . . . ' — 'African Incident' (8/14)
'Pass me the finger-bowl, Moriarty' — 'The Thing on the Mountain' (8/15)
'Keep still . . . ' — 'The Childe Harolde Rewarde' (9/6)
'Now, which of all these fishbones . . . ' — 'The Call of the West' (9/12)

p.93   ''Ere, you two men . . . ' — 'Dishonoured' (5/12) *and* 'Dishonoured — Again' (9/13)
'Any fear of *work* today?' — 'World War One' (8/22)
'What does *that* mean?' — 'The Mountain Eaters' (9/5)

p.94   'I'm Only a Strolling Vagabond' from the musical play 'Cousin from Nowhere' by Kunneke: sung in 'China Story' (5/17)
'More Coal!' — 'Crazy People', programme 15.

p.95   'Ooh, I could *spit*!' — 'Ye Bandit of Sherwood Forest' (5/14)
'What am I doin' in *this* army . . . ' — 'Rommel's Treasure' (6/6)
''Twas in the year 1884 . . . ' — 'The History of Communications' (4/18)

p.96   'You know, that's the sort of thing I'd do . . . ' — 'Under Two Floorboards' (5/18)

p.98   'This is the BBC Home Service . . . ' — 'The White Box of Great Bardfield' (5/25)

100

II

GOONOGRAPHY

CONTENTS

Stephens.

INTRODUCTION

The chaos which surrounds the fictional characters in 'The Goon Show' has had a tendency to spill over into real life and affect anyone associated with the shows. The history of the programme is confused and often contradictory. The BBC's files have been thoroughly complicated by last-minute changes of cast, changes of title, and other incidents; and people who were involved with the shows occasionally say things in interviews and articles which suggest that their memory is playing tricks on them — hardly surprising at this distance in time. It is with the hope of clearing up as much of this confusion as possible that this Goonography has been undertaken.

Researching the details proved to be something of a Goon Show in itself, sorting through microfilmed files and scripts at the BBC, ploughing through the *Radio Times*, and, where possible, checking against recordings of the shows themselves. In research of this complexity there is always the chance that small details will go astray; the reader's indulgence is asked for any errors which may have crept in.

An explanation of the BBC's programme filing system is perhaps necessary. When the original recordings were made, they were kept for transmission and subsequent repeats in 'Recorded Programmes Current Library', and were given identification numbers which have been quoted in the chronological index. These are the numbers beginning SLO, TLO, and so on. None of the original recordings still exists under these numbers. Some were transferred to 'Recorded Programmes Permanent Library' (better known as Sound Archives) under new numbers. Those preserved in this way are detailed in Appendix 3.

It is a popular myth that the BBC keeps all its programmes. This would be impossible, as a building the area of W1 would be required to house them all. Sound Archives exists to preserve a representative sample of programmes, and in fact 'The Goon Show' is fairly generously represented — 41 programmes out of 241 ('ITMA' is represented by 44 out of 312, for example). However, 129 shows are preserved in the Transcription Services issues for use by overseas radio stations (and in fact the 1975 series of repeats was drawn entirely from Transcription Services' library).

The main part of this Goonography is a chronological index of all the shows, with their titles, transmission dates, cast changes, and other relevant information. It is preceded by an alphabetical index covering both official and announced titles (where these are different), and followed by appendices dealing with, among other things, the Transcription Services issues, the shows in Archives, and non-Goon-Show appearances by the Goons.

It would have been impossible for me to have compiled all this information without the help I received. My colleagues Tim Smith and Peter Copeland acted as research assistants; Dennis Main Wilson, Peter Eton, John Browell, Bobby Jaye, Ron Belchier, David Allen, Brian Willey, George Martin and Norma Farnes kindly answered silly questions over the telephone. BBC Sound Archives, Script Library, Registry (Radio and Television), Programme Index, Transcription Services and Written Archives Centre at Caversham, and many other departments, were most helpful in providing access to their files and in checking details, as was the British Film Institute. My thanks to all of them.

R. F. Wilmut
December, 1975

CAST LIST

So many characters appeared in the Goon Shows that it is impossible to list them all; all the major characters are included and many of the minor ones, but not those who appeared in one show only. A few minor characters were played by different people from time to time — they are listed under the artist who usually plays them.

HARRY SECOMBE plays
Neddie Seagoon
Fred Bogg (cockney idiot)
Big Chief Worri Guts

Old Uncle Oscar
Mr. Nugent Dirt

PETER SELLERS plays
Mr. Henry Crun
Hercules Grytpype-Thynne
Major Dennis Bloodnok
Bluebottle
Willium ('Mate')
Lew/'Cash'/Judge Schnorrer
Gravely Headstone
Flowerdew ('camp' voice)
Dr. Justin Eidelburger
Reuben Croucher
William J. MacGoonigal (sometimes)

Cynthia/'Breathy Kensington Dear'
Hern (American Announcer)
Babu Banerjee
'Dear Duchess'
Hairy Scot
'Swede' (rustic voice)
'Geraldo'
'Cyril' ('I *seen* 'im')
'Dimbleby'
'Churchill'
and the piano (very badly)

SPIKE MILLIGAN plays
Eccles
Miss Minnie Bannister

Count Jim Moriarty
Throat/MissThroat
Yakamoto
Jim Spriggs
Adolphus Spriggs (wandering singer)
Little Jim

'Wolfit' (tragic actor)
Fred Fu-Manchu (and other fiendish Chinese gentlemen)
Abdul/Singhiz Thingz
Mr. Lalkaka
Bowser (upper-class twit)
Basil (upper-upper-class twit)
William J. MacGoonigal (other times)
Odium

RAY ELLINGTON plays
Big Chief Ellinga
Gladys

The Red Bladder

ALPHABETICAL INDEX

Official titles are indexed to series and number, or date if out-of-series. Transcription Services (TS) and announced titles which differ from the official title are referred to that title.

In the case of announced titles, only the announcement at the beginning of the show is considered, not that after the musical items (unless the show is episodic).

Third series shows are indexed by their official title only.

Some announced titles merely add 'Great' to the official title (e.g., 'The *Great* Spon Plague')— this has been ignored for the purposes of this index; if a title cannot be found, try removing 'Great' from it (or, in some cases, adding it: 'The Tuscan Salami Scandal' is correctly 'The Great Tuscan Salami Scandal').

    * indicates announced title differing from official one.
  ** indicates TS title differing from official one.
   + indicates announcement for *part* of a show (other than 3rd series).
  V = 'Vintage Goons' (after 8th series in main list).

CHRONOLOGICAL INDEX

This index comprises a complete chronological listing of the ten broadcast series, together with the 'Vintage Goons' series recorded for Transcription Services concurrently with the 8th series, and the specials such as 'Cinderella', 'The Starlings', 'The Reason Why' and 'Archie in Goonland'. Short contributions to other programmes are also included if they were recorded during Goon Show sessions, but appearances by the Goons in other programmes and on television are listed in Appendix 4, which also includes 'The Last Goon Show of All', and other appearances since the Goon Shows proper finished in 1960.
The Chronological Index is laid out as follows:

PAGE HEADINGS: Producer, script credits, day of broadcast and pre-recording, and changes of cast applicable to the whole series. The script credits are given as in the official documentation; in fact it seems likely that Larry Stephens made at least some contribution to many of the scripts credited to Milligan alone, and that some of the scripts listed as collaborations were largely Milligan's work. In general, Stephens's plots tend to have a beginning, a middle, and an end; whereas Milligan's tend to have a middle. . . .

SHOW-BY-SHOW DETAILS

SERIES NUMBER: Straight numerical listing within each series. Some BBC files list cumulative numbers; these get progressively more inaccurate.

TRANSMISSION DATE: Date of first transmission *only*. All first transmissions were on Home Service except 'The Goons Hit Wales' (Light Programme 1-3-56). and 'Operation Christmas Duff' (General Overseas Service, 24-12-56). Most in-series shows were repeated a few days after the first placing, usually on Light Programme. Many shows also went out on the General Overseas Service. None of these repeats has been listed. There were also a number of repeats between series, and since the shows ended; for details of these see Appendix 1. To facilitate the repeats on Light Programme, most shows from the 6th series on had separate Light Programme announcements pre-recorded and cut into the tape after the first transmission to replace the Home Service identifications.

RECORDING NUMBER: Reference number of the original recording—made over landline, usually at Broadcasting House, from the outside studio (the Playhouse Theatre, the Camden Theatre, etc.).
    SLO $33^1/_3$ r.p.m. coarse groove 16″ disk recorded at Broadcasting House.
    SBU ditto recorded at Bush House.
    SOX ditto recorded at 200 Oxford Street.
    TLO=15 i.p.s. tape recorded at Broadcasting House.
    TBUditto recorded at Bush House.
    TNCditto recorded in Newcastle (!)

TITLE: The title given here is the official BBC title; references are given to the notes on the page opposite. Transcription Services have adopted different titles for several shows; these have been shown adjacent to the original title. The first two series do not have titles, as the shows are episodic.

ADDITIONAL INFORMATION: Changes of cast for individual shows (mostly the addition of guest artists) and recording dates other than the previous Sunday are also shown. Except where noted, the shows are nominally half an hour long, usually with about a minute and a half of playout to bring the duration to just over thirty minutes.

NOTES

Notes to each series (except the first two, which do not require detailed notes) are on the page opposite each series listing. Announced titles which differ from the official title have been detailed, together with any other relevant information.

NOTE 1 indicates throughout that the show is not announced by any coherent title (except, of course, as 'The Goon Show'); for the purposes of these notes, only announcements at or near the beginnings of the show are being considered, not those after the musical items. The 3rd series shows are not included in this, as the titles given do not usually apply to the first sketch, which often does not have a title in any case. Those 4th series shows which are episodic have been detailed in the notes; there is usually no very coherent title given to the first episode in these shows.

TECHNICAL CREDITS

The technical work in the studio is divided as follows; 'Panel' Studio Manager (balance and control—the term derives from 'mixing panel', the old-fashioned name for the studio desk); 'Grams' SM (playing pre-recorded effects on disk and tape, as well as gramophone records); and 'Spot Effects' SM (live effects in the studio).

It has not been possible to assemble full show-by-show credits for the technical staff who worked on the Goon Shows over the years, as no official records have been kept (apart from occasional credits on the fronts of scripts, and in a few closing announcements at the ends of series); and at this remove those involved cannot remember accurately which shows they worked on. The information which follows lists the main team of Studio Managers for each series, but in some cases members of this team were replaced owing to leave, sickness, etc.

1st series	—no details available; it appears that there was no regular team.	
2nd series	—'technical supervision' of the series (i.e. panel SM) is credited to Keith Fell in the closing announcement of the last show.	
3rd, 4th & 5th series	—Panel	—John Browell (who later produced the 9th and 10th series)
	Grams	—Ian Cook
	Spot	—John Hamilton (David Allen on some shows)
'The Starlings'	—Panel	—Harry Green
	Grams	—Barry Wilson, assisted by Ron Belchier
6th, 7th & 8th series	—Panel	—Bobby Jaye
	Grams	—Ian Cook
	Spot	—Ron Belchier
9th series	—Panel	—Brian Willey
	Grams	—Ian Cook
	Spot	—Jimmy Pope
10th series	—Panel	—Brian Willey
	Grams	—Ian Cook
	Spot	—Harry Morriss

1st Series

Billed as: 'CRAZY PEOPLE, featuring Radio's own Crazy Gang — "The Goons".'
With Peter Sellers, Harry Secombe, Spike Milligan, Michael Bentine, The Ray Ellington Quartet, The Stargazers, Max Geldray, and (except where stated) the BBC Dance Orchestra, conducted by Stanley Black. Announcer Andrew Timothy, except nos. 8-10, announcer Denys Drower.
Scripts written by Spike Milligan and Larry Stephens, edited by Jimmy Grafton. Produced by Dennis Main Wilson, except 11-14, produced by Leslie Bridgmont. Nos. 1-9 broadcast on Mondays, nos. 10-17 on Thursdays. All pre-recorded the previous Sunday.
The shows consist of four or five short sketches separated by musical items.

1	28- 5-51	SLO 90268	
2	4- 6-51	SLO 90269	
3	11- 6-51	SLO 90452	
4	18- 6-51	SLO 90366	
5	25- 6-51	SOX 59949	
6	2- 7-51	SLO 91295	
			(with the BBC Revue Orch. cond. by Robert Busby)
7	9- 7-51	SLO 91565	(with the BBC Revue Orch. cond. by Robert Busby)
8	16- 7-51	SLO 92262	
9	23- 7-51	SLO 92468	
10	2- 8-51	SLO 92867	
11	9- 8-51	SOX 61088*	
12	16- 8-51	SLO 93368	
13	23- 8-51	SOX 61088*	
14	30- 8-51	SLO 93400	
15	6- 9-51	SBU 71149	
16	13- 9-51	SLO 94892	(with the BBC Revue Orch. cond. by Robert Busby)
17	20- 9-51	SLO 95143	(without Geldray, with Marie Benson (vocalist) and the Skyrockets Orch. cond. by Woolf Phillips)
SP	26-12-51	SLO 99928	CINDERELLA (pantomime) with Lizbeth Webb as Cinderella, Graham Stark as Prince Charming: The Goons: The Stargazers: The Ray Ellington Quartet: Max Geldray and the Augmented Dance Orchestra conducted by Stanley Black. Produced by Dennis Main Wilson. Recorded 16-12-51

* obviously these shows can't both have had the same number, but it has not been possible to cross-check any further the information given in those official files which still exist.

116

2nd Series

Billed as 'THE GOON SHOW, featuring those crazy people. . . .'
Cast and musicians as for the previous series for the first six shows, after which the Stargazers left.
Scripts by Spike Milligan and Larry Stephens, edited by Jimmy Grafton (who also wrote special lyrics for some shows).
Produced by Dennis Main Wilson.
Broadcast Tuesdays, pre-recorded the previous Sunday (except nos. 24 & 25).

1	22-1-52	SLO 1768	
2	29-1-52	SLO 2147	
3	5-2-52	SLO 2519	
	12-2-52		No transmission owing to the death of King George VI
4	19-2-52	SLO 3334	(BBC Dance Orch. cond. by Stanley Andrews)
5	26-2-52	SLO 3627	
6	4-3-52	SLO 4021	
7	11-3-52	SLO 4179	
8	18-3-52	SLO 5112	The Goons' version of Rider Haggard's 'She'— entitled 'Her'*
9	25-3-52	SLO 5277	
10	1-4-52	SLO 5380	
11	8-4-52	SLO 5684	(without Milligan)
12	15-4-52	SLO 6306	
13	22-4-52	SLO 6737	
14	29-4-52	SLO 6959	
15	6-5-52	SBU 83555	
16	13-5-52	SLO 7761	
17	20-5-52	SLO 8202	
18	27-5-52	SLO 8179	
19	3-6-52	SLO 9302	(with the BBC Revue Orch. cond. by Robert Busby)
20	10-6-52	SLO 9307	(with the BBC Dance Orch. cond. by Wally Stott)
21	17-6-52	SLO 9638	(without Bentine)
22	24-6-52	SLO 9955	
23	1-7-52	SLO 10474	
24	8-7-52	SLO 11378	(recorded 29-6-52)
25	15-7-52	SLO 10808	(recorded 6-7-52)

* this is the first in-series show to have a single plot lasting right through the programme.

3rd Series

From now on billed as 'THE GOON SHOW'.
Basic cast—Sellers, Secombe, Milligan, with Geldray, Ellington and orchestra conducted by Wally Stott. Announcer Andrew Timothy. Bentine has now left.
Produced by Peter Eton, except 18 & 19 produced by Charles Chilton.
Scripts by Spike Milligan and Larry Stephens, edited by Jimmy Grafton.
All except 7 broadcast Tuesdays: pre-recorded the previous Sunday (except 20-22).
The shows have 3 parts; the title given is usually that of the middle episode.

1	11-11-52	SLO 17297	Fred of the Islands[2]
2	18-11-52	SOX 82948	The Egg of the Great Auk[3]
3	25-11-52	SLO 18332	I Was a Male Fan Dancer[2]
4	2-12-52	SLO 18613	The Saga of HMS Aldgate[2]
5	9-12-52	SLO 18848	The Expedition for Toothpaste[4] (without Milligan)
6	16-12-52	SLO 19414	The Archers[2] (without Milligan)
7	26-12-52	SLO 19526	Robin Hood[5] (Christmas Pantomime—45 minutes: without Milligan; with Dick Emery & Carole Carr)
8	30-12-52	SLO 19783	Where Does Santa Claus Go in the Summer?[6] (without Milligan, with Ellis Powell)
9	6- 1-53	SLO 20338	The Navy, Army, and Air Force[2] (without Milligan, with Dick Emery)
10	13- 1-53	SLO 20695	The British Way of Life[2] (without Milligan, with Graham Stark)
11	20- 1-53	SLO 20948	A Survey of Britain[2] (without Milligan, with Dick Emery)
12	27- 1-53	SLO 21647	Flint of the Flying Squad[2] (without Milligan, with Graham Stark)
13	3- 2-53	SOX 86757	Seaside Resorts in Winter[2] (without Milligan, with Dick Emery)
14	10- 2-53	SLO 22493	The Tragedy of Oxley Towers[3] (without Milligan, with Graham Stark & Valentine Dyall)
15	17- 2-53	SLO 22860	The Story of Civilization[7] (without Milligan, with Dick Emery)
16	24- 2-53	SLO 22973	The Search for the Bearded Vulture[3] (without Milligan, with Graham Stark)
17	3- 3-53	SLO 23540	The Mystery of the Monkey's Paw[8] (Milligan returns; with Dick Emery)
18	10- 3-53	SLO 24224	The Mystery of the Cow on the Hill[9]
19	17- 3-53	SLO 24432	Where Do Socks Come From?[3]
	24- 3-53		No transmission owing to the death of Queen Mary
20	31- 3-53	SLO 24764	The Man Who Never Was[10] (recorded 22-3-53)
21	7- 4-53	SLO 25520	The Building of the Suez Canal[3] (recorded 29-3-53)
22	14- 4-53	SLO 25873	The De Goonlies[3] (recorded 5-4-53)
23	21- 4-53	SLO 26517	The Conquest of Space[2]
24	28- 4-53	SLO 26797	The Ascent of Mount Everest[3]
25	5- 5-53	SLO 27952	The Story of the Plymouth Hoe Armada[3]
SP	3- 6-53	SLO 29390	Coronation edition[11] (40 minutes; recorded 1-6-53; without Geldray; with Graham Stark)

The titles given (with one exception) are taken from the fronts of the scripts in BBC Script Library, where they have been pencilled in. In most cases the title is applicable to the middle section of the show (details are given below). As these shows are episodic any titling is bound to be somewhat arbitrary, but it should be emphasized that, from the point of view of the listener, this series would not be regarded as having titles, still being in the traditional variety format.

2. Title given is that of middle part of show.
3. Title given is that of parts 2 *and* 3 of show.
4. At this point Milligan went into hospital suffering from a nervous breakdown. This show and the next had already been written; after a few weeks Milligan resumed writing the shows in collaboration with Larry Stephens. The title given here is of the middle sketch, which later re-appeared in the 20th of the 4th series.
5. This show, which has a straight-through plot, is credited on the front of the script to 'Thomas Alcock & William Bull (from the original Alcock and Bull story)'. It was in fact mostly written by Jimmy Grafton (working for 36 hours continuously!), Milligan being in hospital and Larry Stephens unwell. The opening few pages were re-used in the 14th of the 5th series.
6. In the absence of an official title, the title of the final sketch has been adopted (the answer being that he stays in Greenland on account of Eskimo Nell). The middle sketch is a re-make, with a few additions, of 'The Archers' (middle part of no. 6 of this series). Ellis Powell, who makes a brief appearance, was the current Mrs. Dale of 'Mrs Dale's Diary'.
7. 'The Story of Civilization', which is the middle episode, is a re-make of part of the 6th of the 1st series.
8. The title given here is of the first sketch; the remainder of the show is 'The Search for Brigadier Winchmold'.
9. The title given here is that of the first sketch; the remainder of the show is 'The Siege of Khartoum', used again in no. 18 of the 4th series.
10. The title given is parts 2 *and* 3; this story appears again, in expanded form, as the 27th of the 6th series, and then again as the 21st of the 8th series.
11. This show, which sticks to one plot the whole way through, purports to present a recorded commentary on the Coronation procession.

4th Series

Scripts 1-9 and 11-20 by Spike Milligan and Larry Stephens; no. 10 by Larry Stephens; remainder by Spike Milligan.
Announcer Andrew Timothy (nos. 1-5); then Wallace Greenslade.
Produced by Peter Eton, except no. 15 produced by Jacques Brown.
Nos. 1-20 (except 13) broadcast on Fridays, nos. 21-30 on Mondays; all pre-recorded the previous Sunday.

1	2-10-53	TLO 35079	The Dreaded Piano Clubber[2]
2	9-10-53	TLO 35432	The Man Who Tried to Destroy London's Monuments[3]
3	16-10-53	TLO 35740	The Ghastly Experiments of Dr. Hans Eidelburger[4]
4	23-10-53	TLO 36235	The Building of Britain's First Atomic Cannon[5]
5	30-10-53	TLO 37145	The Gibraltar Story[6]
6	6-11-53	TLO 37511	Through the Sound Barrier in an Airing Cupboard[1]
7	13-11-53	TLO 37898	The First Albert Memorial to the Moon
8	20-11-53	TLO 38482	The Missing Bureaucrat[7]
9	27-11-53	TLO 37891	Operation Bagpipes
10	4-12-53	TLO 39091	The Flying Saucer Mystery[8]
11	11-12-53	TLO 39790	The Spanish Armada[9]
12	18-12-53	TLO 40412	The British Way
SP	25-12-53	TLO 40660	Short insert in 'Christmas Crackers' (which also contained contributions from other Variety shows) (recorded 20-12-53)
13	26-12-53	TLO 40660	The Giant Bombardon (with Michael Bentine)
14	1- 1-54	TLO 40965	Ten Thousand Fathoms Down in a Wardrobe
15	8- 1-54	TLO 41242	The Missing Prime Minister
16	15- 1-54	TLO 41552	Dr. Jekyll and Mr. Crun[10]
17	22- 1-54	TLO 42416	The Mummified Priest
18	29- 1-54	TLO 42842	The History of Communications[11]
19	5- 2-54	TLO 48011	The Kippered Herring Gang
20	12- 2-54	TLO 49072	The Toothpaste Expedition[12]
21	15- 2-54	TLO 49191	The Case of the Vanishing Room
22	22- 2-54	TLO 49628	The Great Ink Drought of 1902[13]
23	1- 3-54	TLO 50206	The Greatest Mountain in the World
24	8- 3-54	TLO 50546	The Collapse of the British Railway Sandwich System
25	15- 3-54	TLO 50871	The Silent Bugler[14]
26	22- 3-54	TLO 51429	Western Story[15]
27	29- 3-54	TLO 51769	The Saga of the Internal Mountain
28	5- 4-54	TLO 52346	The Invisible Acrobat[16] (Ellington pre-recorded)
29	12- 4-54	TLO 52583	The Great Bank of England Robbery (Ellington pre-recorded)
30	19- 4-54	TLO 52599	The Siege of Fort Knight (Ellington pre-recorded)
SP	11- 6-54	TLO 55169	ARCHIE IN GOONLAND with Peter Brough and Archie Andrews, Peter Sellers, Spike Milligan, Harry Secombe, Hattie Jacques, and the BBC Variety Orchestra, conductor Paul Fenoulhet. Script by Eric Sykes and Spike Milligan. Produced by Roy Speer. Recorded 6-5-54

With this series, the shows begin for the first time to take on the familiar dramatic format, although it is not until the second half of the series that the majority of the shows have a straight-through half-hour plot (apart from the musical items, of course). As yet the shows were not given titles at the time of writing, with the result that the situation has become rather confused. Spike Milligan has titled his own copies of the scripts with abbreviated titles that are really more of a shorthand indication of the content. Someone has written in pencil on the fronts of the BBC Script Library copies titles which tend to be based on the opening announcements; however, as many of the shows have a short opening sketch with the main part of the programme starting only after the first musical items, these titles tend to be misleading.

The titles given in the list opposite are derived from both sources, with a tendency to use Milligan's titles where there is a choice between two reasonably acceptable alternatives. Only one show in this series has been preserved in BBC Sound Archives (no. 23); in this case the BBC title has been retained in preference to Milligan's.

1. Not coherently announced.
2. Three-episode show; the middle section is 'The Dreaded Piano Clubber'.
3. This story occupies the second and third episodes of the show.
4. The first part of the show is 'The Adventures of Fearless Harry Secombe', a 'serial' which appears at the start of several shows; the title given for the show is the subtitle of this first section. The remainder of the show is about the ascent of Mount Everest.
5. Announced as title. This is the first show in this series to have a single plot lasting through all three parts.
6. The title given applies to parts 2 and 3.
7. The first part of the show is 'The Further Adventures of Fearless Harry Secombe — A Race to the Death'. 'The Missing Bureaucrat' is parts 2 and 3.
8. The first part of the show is again 'The Adventures of Fearless Harry Secombe' (the title given on the BBC Script Library copy); however, the main part of the show is about flying saucers, and as Spike Milligan's copy of the script is missing and therefore no title has been given for it, I have taken the liberty of inventing a title.
9. In the first part of the show 'Harry Proves he is Not a Dog'; parts 2 and 3 are the story of the Armada.
10. Announced as 'Crime Does Not Pay Income Tax'.
11. Part one of the script is 'The History of Communications', originally part of the 7th of the 1st series and later re-worked into 'The GPO Show'. Parts 2 and 3 are 'The Siege of Khartoum', originally part of the 18th of the 3rd series.
12. The first part of the script was originally used in the 2nd of the 2nd series; 'The Toothpaste Expedition' was originally used in the 5th of the 3rd series.
13. Announced as 'Hansard Unexpurgated'.
14. The nearest to an announcement is 'take the case of Agent X2 . . .'.
15. Announced as 'Brain!' (inspired by the film, *Shane*).
16. Announced as 'Bulletto'.

Fourteen of these scripts were re-worked for the 'Vintage Goons' series recorded in 1957/8 for Transcription Services.

SP 31- 8-54 TNC 408 THE STARLINGS
Peter Sellers, Harry Secombe, Spike Milligan and
Andrew Timothy. Written by Spike Milligan.
Without musicians or audience.
Produced by Peter Eton. Recorded 11/12-8-54

5th Series

From now on the announcer is Wallace Greenslade.
Scripts for shows 1-6 by Spike Milligan, remainder by Milligan and Eric Sykes.
Produced by Peter Eton.
Broadcast Tuesdays, pre-recorded the previous Sunday, except nos. 14 and 20.

1	28- 9-54	TLO 62960	The Whistling Spy Enigma
2	5-10-54	TLO 63962	The Lost Gold Mine (of Charlotte)[2]
3	12-10-54	TLO 64018	The Dreaded Batter-Pudding Hurler (of Bexhill-on-Sea)[3]
4	19-10-54	TLO 64443	The Phantom Head Shaver (of Brighton)
5	26-10-54	TLO 64692	The Affair of the Lone Banana
6	2-11-54	TLO 65467	The Canal (with Valentine Dyall)
7	9-11-54	TLO 65972	Lurgi Strikes Britain[1] (TS: Lurgi Strikes Again)
8	16-11-54	TLO 67106	The Mystery of the Marie Celeste (Solved)
9	23-11-54	TLO 67320	The Last Tram (from Clapham)
10	30-11-54	TLO 67468	The Booted Gorilla (found?)
11	7-12-54	TLO 68322	The Spanish Suitcase[1]
12	14-12-54	TLO 68149	Dishonoured, or The Fall of Neddie Seagoon
13	21-12-54	TLO 69220	Forog
14	28-12-54	TLO 69221	Ye Bandit of Sherwood Forest (recorded 19-12-54: with Charlotte Mitchell)
15	4- 1-55	TLO 70044	Nineteen-Eighty-Five[5] (orch. cond. by Bruce Campbell)
16	11- 1-55	TLO 70045	The Case of the Missing Heir[1]
17	18- 1-55	TLO 70610	China Story
18	25- 1-55	TLO 72116	Under Two Floorboards — A Story of the Legion[1]
19	1- 2-55	TLO 71797	The Missing Scroll[4]
20	8- 2-55	TLO 71798	Nineteen-Eighty-Five[5] (recorded 30-1-55: with John Snagge — pre-rec.)
21	15- 2-55	TLO 72450	The Sinking of Westminster Pier[6]
22	22- 2-55	TLO 72538	The Fireball of Milton Street[7]
23	1- 3-55	TLO 73044	The Six Ingots of Leadenhall Street[8]
24	8- 3-55	TLO 73495	Yehti
25	15- 3-55	TLO 74145	The White Box of Great Bardfield[1]
26	22- 3-55	TLO 74489	The End[9] (TS: — reissue only: Confessions of a Secret Senna-pod Drinker)

With the beginning of this series, the first to be taken by the BBC Transcription
Services, the shows become the familiar and well-remembered full-length stories,
featuring by now most of the best-known characters. This is the only series honoured
by *Radio Times* with a synopsis and cast list for most shows (although these get
progressively more divorced from reality as the series wears on).

.   Not coherently announced.
.   Announced as 'Death in the Desert'.
.   Announced as 'The Terror of Bexhill-on-Sea'.
.   Announced as 'The Lost Music of Purdom'.
.   Inspired by Nigel Kneale's television adaptation of Orwell's *1984*. The show was
    such a success that the script was repeated by popular demand: the second
    appearance is not a recorded repeat but a new performance of the script,
    which was re-typed, incorporating all but one of the timing cuts made for the
    first version. In the second show Snagge (pre-recorded) reads the telescreen
    announcement near the beginning: in the original this is read by Sellers.
.   Billed in *Radio Times* (and Programme Index) as 'The Six Ingots of Leadenhall
    Street'; the script was changed at short notice to a story inspired by the appear-
    ance of a photograph of the floating pier at Westminster under several feet of
    water with an 'Out of Order' notice being pinned to it. Greenslade tries to
    announce the show as 'The Six Ingots of Leadenhall Street' (insisting that the
    Radio Times is never wrong): finally Sellers announces it as 'The Port of London
    Authority's valuable hand-carved, oil-painted, valuable floating pier'.
.   'Milton Street' is the name of a village in Sussex.
.   The title situation for this show can best be described as confusing. The front of
    the script, *Radio Times*, Programme Index and the 'Programme as Broadcast'
    files give the title as 'The Terrible Blasting of Moreton's Bank'. However, the
    show is in fact 'The Six Ingots of Leadenhall Street', the script postponed from
    15-2-55 (see note 6), is announced as such, and titled as such by TS. Strictly
    speaking, the title opposite ought to match the official files; but since the 'Six
    Ingots' title makes more sense, and in fact would have been the official title of
    the script had not the last-minute change of plan happened, I have decided to
    adopt it.
.   Announced as 'The Confessions of a Secret Senna-pod Drinker'.

6th Series

Scripts by Spike Milligan (SM) except where indicated; ES=Eric Sykes, LS=Larr Stephens.
Produced by Peter Eton (nos. 1-21) and Pat Dixon (nos. 22-27).
Broadcast Tuesdays, pre-recorded the previous Sunday (except nos. 10 & 15).

1	20- 9-55	TLO 86722	The Man Who Won the War[2] (SM & ES) (TS Seagoon MCC)
2	27- 9-55	TLO 87028	The Secret Escritoire (SM & ES)
3	4-10-55	TLO 87493	The Lost Emperor[1]
4	11-10-55	TLO 88253	Napoleon's Piano[3]
5	18-10-55	TLO 88477	The Case of the Missing CD Plates[4]
6	25-10-55	TLO 88977	Rommel's Treasure[5]
7	1-11-55	TLO 89727	Foiled by President Fred[6]
8	8-11-55	TLO 90136	Shangri-La Again[7]
9	15-11-55	TBU 52103	The International Christmas Pudding[8]
	22-11-55		(No. 10 postponed to 3-4-56,[9] replaced by repeat o 'China Story', first broadcast 18-1-55)
11	29-11-55	TLO 91637	The Sale of Manhattan[10] (TS: The Lost Colony)
12	6-12-55	TLO 92346	The Terrible Revenge of Fred Fu-Manchu[11]
SP	8-12-55	TLO 92849	The Missing Christmas Parcel — Post Early for Christ mas (ES) (15 minutes — broadcast in Children's Hour recorded 27-11-55: without musicians). Devised an produced by Peter Eton and John Lane
13	13-12-55	TLO 93483	The Lost Year
14	20-12-55	TLO 93839	The Greenslade Story (with John Snagge)
15	27-12-55	TLO 93838	The Hastings Flyer — Robbed[12] (recorded 18-12-55)
16	3- 1-56	TLO 94673	The Mighty Wurlitzer
17	10- 1-56	TLO 94832	The Raid of the International Christmas Pudding[1]
18	17- 1-56	TLO 95608	Tales of Montmartre (SM & ES) (with Charlott Mitchell)
19	24- 1-56	TLO 95990	The Jet-Propelled Guided NAAFI[1]
20	31- 1-56	TLO 96271	The House of Teeth[1] (with Valentine Dyall)
21	7- 2-56	TLO 97228	Tales of Old Dartmoor (orch. cond. by Bruc Campbell)
22	14- 2-56	TLO 97297	The Choking Horror (orch. cond. by Bruc Campbell)
23	21- 2-56	TLO 98295	The Great Tuscan Salami Scandal[13] (without musi cians, with John Snagge — pre-rec.)
24	28- 2-56	TLO 98661	The Treasure in the Lake[14] (orch. cond. Bruc Campbell)
SP	1- 3-56	TLO 98662	The Goons Hit Wales (5½ minute insert in St. David's Day programme, recorded 26-2-56)
25	6- 3-56	TLO 98778	The Fear of Wages[15] (SM & LS)
26	13- 3-56	TLO 98950	Scradje (SM & LS) (with John Snagge — pre-rec.)
27	20- 3-56	TLO 99481	The Man Who Never Was[16] (SM & LS)
10	3- 4-56	TLO 90647	The Pevensey Bay Disaster[9] (recorded 20-11-55)
SP	29- 8-56	TLO 11466	China Story (SM & ES)[17] (recorded 24-8-56 at the National Radio Show. Produced by Dennis Main Wilson)

1. Not coherently announced.
2. Announced as 'Seagoon MCC' (because he was a batman . . .).
3. The script and the Programme Index entry are wrongly titled 'The Sale of Manhattan'.
4. Announced as 'A Strange Case of Diplomatic Immunity'.
5. Announced as 'The Search for Rommel's Treasure'.
6. Announced as 'In Honour Bound'.
7. Announced as 'Lost Horizon'.
8. Announced as 'The Great International Christmas Pudding'.
9. On the day the show was recorded there was a serious train crash at Didcot in which 10 people were killed and 116 injured. In view of the fact that the show contains a train crash, the broadcast was cancelled and replaced with a repeat of 'China Story' from the previous series. (See 'The Hastings Flyer — Robbed'[12]).
10. Announced as 'The Lost Colony'.
11. Announced as 'Fred Fu-Manchu and his Bamboo Saxophone'.
12. This script is identical to that for 'The Pevensey Bay Disaster' (see note 9), incorporating the timing cuts made for that occasion; only the announcements are changed, to 'The Hastings Flyer'. The earlier version of the show is the one issued by TS, as they recorded directly by line from the studio, so that to them 'The Hastings Flyer' was a repeat. 'The Pevensey Bay Disaster' was eventually broadcast two weeks after the end of the series, so that to the British listeners 'The Hastings Flyer' is the original version.
13. There was a musicians' strike on at the time. In common with other Variety shows, the cast made do without music. This show and the next also include Milligan's famous ballad 'I'm Walking Backwards for Christmas'. The programme is not coherently announced.
14. Announced as 'The Treasure of Loch Lomond'.
15. Inspired by the film 'The Wages of Fear'.
16. This is an expanded version of the script which formed parts 2 & 3 of the 20th of the 3rd series. It appears again in the 8th series.
17. This is a new production of no. 17 of the 5th series—the script is almost identical.

7th Series

Scripts by Milligan and Larry Stephens, except nos. 2 and 23, by Milligan only.
Produced by Pat Dixon, except nos. 1 and 2 produced by Peter Eton.
Broadcast Thursdays, except nos. 10 and 13 broadcast Wednesdays.
Pre-recorded the previous Sunday (except nos. 6, 14, 15 and 16).

1	4-10-56	TLO 12681	The Nasty Affair at the Burami Oasis[1]
2	11-10-56	TLO 11799	Drums Along the Mersey (with Valentine Dyall)
3	18-10-56	TLO 14585	The Nadger Plague[2]
4	25-10-56	TLO 14586	The MacReekie Rising of '74 (without Milligan, with George Chisholm)
5	1-11-56	TLO 15209	The Spectre of Tintagel (with Valentine Dyall)
	8-11-56		(no. 6 postponed to 14-2-57[3]; replaced by repeat of 'The Greenslade Story', first broadcast 20-12-55)
7	15-11-56	TLO 15801	The Great Bank Robbery
8	22-11-56	TLO 16600	Personal Narrative[4]
9	29-11-56	TLO 16989	The Mystery of the Fake Neddie Seagoons[5] (TS: The Case of the Fake Neddie Seagoons)
SP	for TS only	TLO 17360	Robin Hood[6] (with Valentine Dyall and Dennis Price) (recorded 2-12-56; not broadcast in Britain)
10	5-12-56	TLO 17361	What's My Line?
11	13-12-56	TLO 17963	The Telephone
12	20-12-56	TLO 18731	The Flea
SP	24-12-56 GOS *only*	TLO 17962	Operation Christmas Duff[7] (special overseas edition — recorded 9-12-56)
13	26-12-56	TLO 19238	Six Charlies in Search of an Author
14	3- 1-57	TLO 19237	Emperor of the Universe (rec. 23-12-56)
15	10- 1-57	TLO 20041	Wings Over Dagenham (rec. 30-12-56) (with George Chisholm)
16	17- 1-57	TLO 20042	The Rent Collectors (rec. 30-12-56) (with Bernard Miles)
17	24- 1-57	TLO 21509	Shifting Sands[1] (with Jack Train[8])
18	31- 1-57	TLO 21793	The Moon Show
19	7- 2-57	TLO 23090	The Mysterious Punch-up-the-Conker[1]
6	14- 2-57	TLO 14930	The Sleeping Prince[3] (recorded 4-11-56)
20	21- 2-57	TLO 22507	Round the World in Eighty Days
21	28- 2-57	TLO 23565	Insurance, the White Man's Burden
22	7- 3-57	TLO 24413	The Africa Ship Canal[9]
23	14- 3-57	TLO 24461	Ill Met by Goonlight
24	21- 3-57	TLO 24999	The Missing Boa Constrictor[1]
25	28- 3-57	TLO 26030	The Histories of Pliny the Elder

1. Not coherently announced.
2. Announced as 'The Great Nadger Plague'.
3. This show, which parodies a Latin-American type revolution, was postpone. owing to the international situation at the time (among other things, the Hungarian uprising was taking place).
4. Announced as 'The Personal Narrative of Captain Neddie Seagoon, R.N.'.
5. Announced as 'The Great Art Mystery, or The Case of the Fake Neddie Seagoon'.
6. Announced as 'Robin Hood and his Mirry Mon'. This show, which was recorded specially for TS and not broadcast in this country (although it has been issued on Parlophone PMC 7132) is partially based on the script originally broadcast 28-12-54 as 'Ye Bandit of Sherwood Forest' (14th of 5th series).
7. The BBC General Overseas Service was at this time broadcasting entirely on short waves, so that this show could only have been heard in this country — and then not very satisfactorily — by listeners equipped with short-wave receivers. The show was aimed largely at the British Armed Forces overseas.
8. As Colonel Chinstrap (from 'ITMA'). It is interesting that the character, although from a different show a decade earlier, fits into the Goon Show framework with no sense of strain.
9. Announced as 'The Great Trans-Africa Canal'.

SP 22- 8-57 TLO 35307 THE REASON WHY
Peter Sellers, Harry Secombe, Spike Milligan, and Valentine Dyall. Announcer Wallace Greenslade. Music pre-recorded: no audience. Produced by Jacques Brown. Recorded 11-8-57

8th Series

Scripts by Spike Milligan (SM), Larry Stephens (LS), John Antrobus (JA), and Maurice Wiltshire (MW), as indicated.
Produced by Charles Chilton (nos. 1-5 & 17-26), Roy Speer (nos. 6-14), and Tom Ronald (nos. 15 & 16).
Broadcast Mondays, pre-recorded the previous Sunday (except no. 18).

1	30- 9-57	TLO 38857	Spon (SM) (without Secombe, with Dick Emery)
2	7-10-57	TLO 39090	* The Junk Affair[1] (SM & LS)
3	14-10-57	TLO 39928	The Burning Embassy[1] (SM & LS)
4	21-10-57	TLO 40052	* The Great Regent's Park Swim (SM & LS)
5	28-10-57	TLO 40562	The Treasure in the Tower[1] (SM & LS)
6	4-11-57	TLO 41101	* The Space Age (SM & LS)
7	11-11-57	TLO 41712	The Red Fort[2] (SM & LS)
8	18-11-57	TLO 41935	* The Missing Battleship[1] (SM & LS) (without Geldray)
9	25-11-57	TLO 42750	The Policy (SM & LS)
10	2-12-57	TLO 42899	* King Solomon's Mines (SM & LS)
11	9-12-57	TLO 43427	The Stolen Postman (LS)
12	16-12-57	TLO 44167	* The Great British Revolution (SM & LS)
13	23-12-57	TLO 44618	The Plasticine Man (SM & LS) (without Ellington)
14	30-12-57	TLO 45270	* African Incident[1] (SM & LS) (with Cécile Chevreau)
15	6- 1-58	TLO 45929	The Thing on the Mountain (LS & MW)
16	13- 1-58	TLO 46344	* The String Robberies[3] (SM) (with George Chisholm)
17	20- 1-58	TLO 47306	The Moriarty Murder Mystery (LS & MW)
18	27- 1-58	TLO 47557	The Curse of Frankenstein[4] (SM) (rec. 19-1-58) (without Ellington, with George Chisholm)
19	3- 2-58	TLO 47740	The White Neddie Trade (LS & MW)
20	10- 2-58	TLO 48542	Ten Snowballs that Shook the World (SM)
21	17- 2-58	TLO 49421	* The Man Who Never Was[5] (SM & LS)
22	24- 2-58	TLO 49663	* World War One[6] (SM) (TS: '____!')
23	3- 3-58	TLO 50040	* The Spon Plague[7] (SM & JA) (with George Chisholm)
24	10- 3-58	TLO 51225	* Tiddleywinks[1] (SM) (with John Snagge)
25	17- 3-58	TLO 50769	* The Evils of Bushey Spon[8] (SM) (with A. E. Matthews)
26	24- 3-58	TLO 51440	* The Great Statue Debate[1] (SM & JA)

* a special TS series of 'Vintage Goons' (based on scripts from the 4th series) was recorded on the same dates as the shows marked* (see page 130).

1. Not coherently announced.
2. Announced as 'A Tale of India'.
3. Announced as 'The Great String Robberies'.
4. Announced as 'The Curse of Frankenstein—BLAST!' and then continues as a story entitled 'My Heart's in the Highlands'.
5. This script is a re-working of no. 27 of the 6th series, itself an expanded version of part of no. 20 of the 3rd series. It is the 6th series version which has been issued by Transcription Services.
6. The script is titled '_____!', as are the TS issues: the announced title is written as '_____!' and pronounced as a faint murmur—Milligan's interpretation of illegible writing on a faded manuscript.
7. Announced as 'The Great Spon Plague'.
8. Inspired by a real-life row A. E. Matthews was having with his local council about a concrete lamp-post they wanted to put outside his house. (There is also a reference to this in the previous show). Mr Matthews appears only in the last five minutes of the show, which are ad-libbed by all concerned owing to Mr Matthews's utter refusal to stick to the plot.

'Vintage Goons'

A series recorded specially for TS.
Scripts by Spike Milligan.
Produced by Charles Chilton (nos. 1, 2, & 9-14), Roy Speer (nos. 3-7), and Tom Ronald (no. 8)
Recorded Sundays together with 8th series shows.

	recorded	TS tape no.	
1	6-10-57	T1/AG/2966	*The Mummified Priest
2	20-10-57	T7/AG/3654	*The Greatest Mountain in the World
3	3-11-57	T1/AG/3054	The Missing Ten Downing Street[2]
4	17-11-57	T5/AG/4309	*The Giant Bombardon (with Valentine Dyall)
5	1-12-57	T5/AG/4341	The Kippered Herring Gang
6	15-12-57	T5/AG/4382	*The Vanishing Room
7	29-12-57	T5/AG/4417	The Ink Shortage[3]
8	12- 1-58	T1/AG/3875	The Mustard and Cress Shortage[4]
9	16- 2-58	T1/AG/3965	The Internal Mountain
10	23- 2-58	T5/AG/4597	The Silent Bugler[5]
11	2- 3-58	T2/AG/4043	*The Great Bank of England Robbery[6]
12	9- 3-58	T1/AG/4025	The Dreaded Piano Clubber
13	16- 3-58	T5/AG/4661	The Siege of Fort Night
14	23- 3-58	T2/AG/4060	*The Albert Memorial[7]

* Six of these shows were broadcast on Mondays immediately prior to the 9th series:

	broadcast	BH tape no.	
1	22- 9-58	TLO 65468	The Mummified Priest
2	29- 9-58	TLO 65469	The Greatest Mountain in the World
4	6-10-58	TLO 65470	The Giant Bombardon
6	13-10-58	TLO 65471	The Vanishing Room
11	20-10-58	TLO 65472	The Great Bank of England Robbery
14	27-10-58	TLO 65473	The Albert Memorial

130

All scripts in this series are based on scripts from the 4th series, often with a certain amount of re-writing. When six of these shows were broadcast in the Home Service immediately prior to the 9th series, *Radio Times* contrived, in a badly-worded write-up, to give the impression that they were recorded repeats of 4th series shows. To add to the confusion, the repeat series broadcast in 1964 and 1970 were billed as 'Vintage Goons', although none of the shows concerned came from the original 'Vintage Goons' series, some of which have still never been broadcast in this country.

2. Based on 4/15 and announced as 'The Missing Prime Minister of 1953'.
3. Based on 4/22 and announced as 'Hansard Unexpurgated'.
4. Based on 4/24 and announced as 'The Collapse of the British Railway Sandwich System'.
5. Based on 4/25; the nearest to an announcement is 'take the Case of Agent X2'
6. Announced first as 'Open Casebook' and later by the official title.
7. Announced as 'The First Albert Memorial to the Moon'.

9th Series

Scripts by Spike Milligan (except no. 7).
Produced by John Browell.
Broadcast Mondays, except no. 12 broadcast Tuesday; pre-recorded previous Sunday.

1	3-11-58	TLO 68887	The Sahara Desert Statue [1]
2	10-11-58	TLO 68950	I Was Monty's Treble
3	17-11-58	TLO 69769	The £1,000,000 Penny [2]
4	24-11-58	TLO 70536	The Pam's Paper Insurance Policy [1]
5	1-12-58	TLO 71336	The Mountain Eaters [1]
6	8-12-58	TLO 71467	The Childe Harolde Rewarde [1]
7	15-12-58	TLO 72138	The Seagoon Memoirs [1] (script by Larry Stephens and Maurice Wiltshire)
8	22-12-58	TLO 72851	Queen Anne's Rain [1]
9	29-12-58	TLO 73413	The Battle of Spion Kop [1]
10	5- 1-59	TLO 74315	Ned's Atomic Dustbin [1] (with John Snagge — pre-rec.)
11	12- 1-59	TLO 75177	Who Is Pink Oboe? [3] (without Sellers; with Kenneth Connor, Valentine Dyall, Graham Stark, Jack Train and John Snagge, (who was pre-rec.))
12	20- 1-59	TLO 76074	The Call of the West [4]
13	26- 1-59	TLO 76177	Dishonoured — Again [5]
14	2- 2-59	TLO 76513	The Scarlet Capsule [6] (with Andrew Timothy — pre-rec.)
15	9- 2-59	TLO 77465	The Tay Bridge [1] (with George Chisholm)
16	16- 2-59	TLO 77725	The Gold Plate Robbery [7]
17	23- 2-59	TLO 78107	The £50 Cure [1] (without Secombe, with Kenneth Connor)

10th Series

Scripts by Spike Milligan.
Produced by John Browell.
Broadcast Thursdays, pre-recorded the previous Sunday.

1	24-12-59	TLO 3710	A Christmas Carol [2]
2	31-12-59	TLO 4230	The Tale of Men's Shirts [3]
3	7- 1-60	TLO 5015	The Chinese Legs [1] (with John Snagge — pre-rec.)
4	14- 1-60	TLO 5454	Robin's Post [4]
5	21- 1-60	TLO 6251	The Silver Dubloons [1] (with Valentine Dyall)
6	28- 1-60	TLO 6786	The Last Smoking Seagoon [5] (with John Snagge — pre-rec.)

1. Not coherently announced.
2. Announced as 'The Story of a Crime-Type Murder'. After the first musical break it becomes 'Ned the Miser'—it is this part which is the story of the £1,000,000 Penny. TS's publicity for their re-issue of this as 'Pick of the Goons' No. 81 wrongly describes it as 'The £1,000 Penny'. Inflation?
3. Announced as 'The Spy, or. . .'. Sellers developed throat trouble shortly before the recording and the other four actors were brought in by John Browell at very short notice. They take the various parts written for Sellers, with minimal re-writing: Dyall replaces Grytpype-Thynne, Connor replaces Willium and a few others, Stark replaces Henry Crun (the Min and Henry episode becomes an Irish couple who are not as successful as the other replacements) and Train, as Colonel Chinstrap, replaces Major Bloodnok.
4. Announced as 'Captain Stingo, or Goon Law, or Anythinggggggg (Hern)'.
5. Announced as 'I Knew Terence Nuke' ('From the book, *I Knew Terence Nuke*, by Eileen Beardsmore-Lewisham, tiddley-doo spot, we present the play, "I Knew Terence Nuke", from the *book* by Eileen Beardsmore-Lewisham'). This show is a new production of the script first broadcast as 'Dishonoured, or The Fall of Neddie Seagoon', 12th of 5th series; there are only slight variations in the text. It is this later version which has been issued on Parlophone PMC 1108, despite their title of 'Dishonoured'.
6. Announced as 'Quatermass O.B.E.'. This show is a parody of the highly successful BBC-TV serial 'Quatermass and the Pit'. Andrew Timothy, who is pre-recorded, reads announcements at the beginning and end of the show that were originally intended to be read by John Snagge.
7. Announced (eventually) as 'The Kleens of Blenchinghall, the story of an ordinary English comedy half-hour'.

1. Not coherently announced.
2. Announced as 'A Merry Christmas and Custard'.
3. Announced as 'Tales of Men's Shirts (a story of down under)'.
4. Announced as 'The Story of Lord Seagoon, Playboy of the Western Approaches'.
5. Announced as 'The Last of the Smoking Seagoons'.

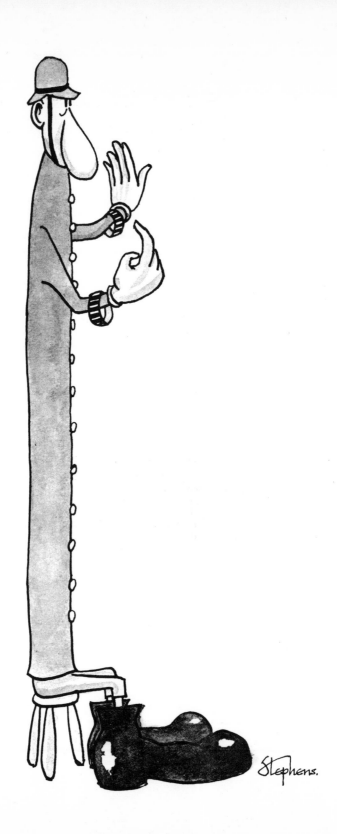

Appendices

1: GOON SHOW REPEATS

The regular in-series repeats are not listed, only additional out-of-series repeats. Dates and series/number references are given.

Nine Goon Shows on Light Programme, Fridays at 1930

29- 4-55	5/1	The Whistling Spy Enigma
6- 5-55	5/2	The Lost Gold Mine (of Charlotte)
13- 5-55	5/4	The Phantom Head Shaver (of Brighton)
20- 5-55	5/5	The Affair of the Lone Banana
27- 5-55	5/6	The Canal
3- 6-55	5/10	The Booted Gorilla (found?)
10- 6-55	5/12	Dishonoured, or The Fall of Neddie Seagoon
17- 6-55	5/17	China Story
24- 6-55	5/22	The Fireball of Milton Street

Replacing 'The Pevensey Bay Disaster' (see 6th series, note 9)
22-11-55	5/17	China Story

Goon Show Special on Home Service, Monday at 1900
2- 1-56	SP	The Starlings

Three Goon Shows on Home Service, Tuesdays at 2030 (2 weeks after end of 6th series)
3- 4-56	6/10	The Pevensey Bay Disaster (first broadcast: this is the same script as 'The Hastings Flyer—Robbed': see 6th series, note 12)
10- 4-56	6/9	The International Christmas Pudding
17- 4-56	6/14	The Greenslade Story

Replacing 'The Great Tuscan Salami Scandal' (see 6th series, note 13) repeat on Light Programme, Sunday at 1530
6- 5-56	6/19	The Jet-Propelled Guided NAAFI

Replacing 'The Sleeping Prince' (see 7th series, note 3)
8-11-56	6/14	The Greenslade Story

Six Goon Shows on Home Service, Thursdays at 2030 (following the 7th series)
4- 4-57	7/1	The Nasty Affair at the Burami Oasis
11- 4-57	7/3	The Nadger Plague
18- 4-57	7/6	The Sleeping Prince
25- 4-57	7/13	Six Charlies in Search of an Author
2- 5-57	7/12	The Flea (broadcast at 2155)
9- 5-57	7/22	The Africa Ship Canal

In series 'The Best of the Best' on Light Programme, Monday at 1931
31- 8-59	9/13	Dishonoured—Again

Seven Goon Shows on Home Service, Thursdays at 1930 (following the 10th series)
4- 2-60	9/3	The £1,000,000 Penny
11- 2-60	9/5	The Mountain Eaters
18- 2-60	9/8	Queen Anne's Rain
25- 2-60	9/12	The Call of the West
3- 3-60	9/16	The Gold Plate Robbery
10- 3-60	9/14	The Scarlet Capsule
17- 3-60	9/13	Dishonoured—Again

In series 'The Best of the Best' on Light Programme, Sunday at 1415
7- 8-60   10/2   The Tale of Men's Shirts

One Goon Show on Home Service, Saturday at 1310
13-10-62   5/3   The Dreaded Batter-Pudding Hurler (of Bexhill-on-Sea)

Nine shows broadcast under the title 'Vintage Goons' (not from the TS series);
Home Service, Fridays at 2130
31- 1-64   6/7   Foiled by President Fred
7- 2-64   7/21   Insurance, the White Man's Burden
14- 2-64   9/8   Queen Anne's Rain
21- 2-64   5/14   Ye Bandit of Sherwood Forest
28- 2-64   8/21   The Man Who Never Was
6- 3-64   9/7   The Seagoon Memoirs
13- 3-64   9/13   Dishonoured — Again
20- 3-64   7/4   The MacReekie Rising of '74
27- 3-64   9/16   The Gold Plate Robbery

In series 'Let's Laugh Again' on Home Service, Friday at 2130
20- 8-65   9/7   The Seagoon Memoirs
                    (the first half of this transmission was marred by a technical
                    fault on the reproducing equipment)

Five Goon Shows on Radio 4, Fridays at 1900
18 - 7-69   5/25   The White Box of Great Bardfield
25- 7-69   5/9   The Last Tram (from Clapham)
1- 8-69   9/5   The Mountain Eaters
8- 8-69   5/7   Lurgi Strikes Britain
15- 8-69   10/6   The Last Smoking Seagoon

One Goon Show on Radio 4, Thursday at 2130
24-12-69   10/1   A Christmas Carol

Eight shows broadcast under the title 'Vintage Goons' (not from the TS series);
Radio 4, Saturdays at 2000
8- 8-70   5/8   The Mystery of the Marie Celeste (Solved)
15- 8-70   5/17   China Story
22- 8-70   5/21   The Sinking of Westminster Pier
29- 8-70   5/24   Yehti
5- 9-70   7/17   Shifting Sands
12- 9-70   6/18   Tales of Montmartre
19- 9-70   8/23   The Spon Plague
26- 9-70   9/2   I Was Monty's Treble

In series 'The Great Shows, 1938-1963', on Radio 2, Sunday at 1430 and Friday at
2002
19-11-72
24-11-72   6/19   The Jet-Propelled Guided NAAFI

Goon Show Special on Radio 4, Bank Holiday Monday at 1345
28- 5-73   SP   The Reason Why

In series 'The Late Show' on Radio 4, Saturday at 2300
9- 3-74   8/16   The String Robberies

In compilation programme 'The Summer Show' on Radio 4, Bank Holiday Monday
at 1130
26- 8-74   5/11   The Spanish Suitcase

136

'Encore the Goons' series on Radio 4, Fridays at 1815 (from TS re-issue versions)

17- 1-75	6/3	The Lost Emperor
24- 1-75	6/25	The Fear of Wages
31- 1-75	7/2	Drums Along the Mersey
7- 2-75	8/10	King Solomon's Mines
14- 2-75	9/6	The Childe Harolde Rewarde
21- 2-75	9/3	The £1,000,000 Penny
28- 2-75	6/9	The International Christmas Pudding
7- 3-75	10/5	The Silver Dubloons
14- 3-75	5/4	The Phantom Head Shaver (of Brighton)
21- 3-75	8/17	The Moriarty Murder Mystery

Starting in 1954, the BBC Transcription Services recorded the Goon Shows for issue on pressed long-playing records to overseas radio stations, who can buy the right to use them for a limited period, usually about two years from the date of issue. The original issues are cut by up to two minutes (topical references and supposedly offensive gags being removed) to run to about 29'30" with some playout. The re-issues ('Pick of the Goons') have further slight cuts, no playout, and, in most cases, a shortened version of the closing signature tune. They all run to 27'00". These records cannot be made available to the public, for contractual reasons.

The shows are listed numerically as issued, with series/number reference.

ORIGINAL ISSUES: 'THE GOON SHOW'

1	5/1	The Whistling Spy Enigma
2	5/2	The Lost Gold Mine
3	5/4	The Phantom Head Shaver
4	5/5	The Affair of the Lone Banana
5	5/6	The Canal
6	5/8	The Mystery of the Marie Celeste — Solved
7	5/12	Dishonoured, or The Fall of Neddie Seagoon
8	5/16	The Case of the Missing Heir
9	5/17	China Story
10	5/18	Under Two Floorboards
11	5/19	The Missing Scroll
12	5/21	The Sinking of Westminster Pier
13	5/26	The End
14	6/4	Napoleon's Piano
15	6/6	Rommel's Treasure
16	6/8	Shangri-La Again
17	6/9	The International Christmas Pudding
18	6/10	The Pevensey Bay Disaster
19	6/11	The Lost Colony (original title 'The Sale of Manhattan')
20	6/13	The Lost Year
21	6/16	The Mighty Wurlitzer
22	6/18	Tales of Montmartre
23	6/5	The Case of the Missing CD Plates
24	6/20	The House of Teeth
25	6/21	Tales of Old Dartmoor
26	6/22	The Choking Horror
27	6/24	The Treasure in the Lake
28	6/23	The Great Tuscan Salami Scandal
29	6/26	Scradje
30	6/27	The Man Who Never Was
31	7/2	Drums Along the Mersey
32	7/4	The MacReekie Rising of '74
33	7/5	The Spectre of Tintagel
34	7/8	Personal Narrative
35	7/9	The Case of the Fake Neddie Seagoons (original title 'The Mystery of the Fake Neddie Seagoons')
36	7/12	The Flea
37	7/13	Six Charlies in Search of an Author
38	7/15	Wings Over Dagenham
39	7/17	Shifting Sands
40	7/18	The Moon Show
41	7/19	The Mysterious Punch-up-the-Conker

42	7/6	The Sleeping Prince

43	7/20	Round the World in Eighty Days
44	7/21	Insurance, the White Man's Burden
45	7/22	The Africa Ship Canal
46	7/23	Ill Met By Goonlight
47	7/24	The Missing Boa Constrictor
48	Special	Robin Hood

49	8/2	The Junk Affair
50	8/4	The Great Regent's Park Swim
51	8/6	The Space Age
52	8/5	The Treasure in the Tower
53	8/8	The Missing Battleship
54	8/9	The Policy
55	8/10	King Solomon's Mines
56	8/11	The Stolen Postman
57	8/12	The Great British Revolution
58	8/13	The Plasticine Man
59	8/14	African Incident
60	8/16	The String Robberies
61	8/17	The Moriarty Murder Mystery
62	8/3	The Burning Embassy
63	8/20	Ten Snowballs that Shook the World
64	8/18	The Curse of Frankenstein
65	8/22	'_____!' (original title 'World War One')
66	8/23	The Spon Plague

67	9/2	I Was Monty's Treble
68	9/3	The £1,000,000 Penny
69	9/4	The Pam's Paper Insurance Policy
70	9/5	The Mountain Eaters
71	9/7	The Seagoon Memoirs
72	9/8	Queen Anne's Rain
73	9/10	Ned's Atomic Dustbin
74	9/6	The Childe Harolde Rewarde
75	9/12	The Call of the West
76	9/14	The Scarlet Capsule
77	9/15	The Tay Bridge
78	9/13	Dishonoured — Again
79	9/16	The Gold Plate Robbery
80	9/17	The £50 Cure

81	10/2	The Tale of Men's Shirts
82	10/3	The Chinese Legs
83	10/4	Robin's Post
84	10/5	The Silver Dubloons
85	10/6	The Last Smoking Seagoon
86	10/1	A Christmas Carol

87	5/14	Ye Bandit of Sherwood Forest
88	5/3	The Dreaded Batter-Pudding Hurler (of Bexhill-on-Sea)
89	5/7	Lurgi Strikes Again (original title 'Lurgi Strikes Britain')
90	5/9	The Last Tram
91	5/10	The Booted Gorilla
92	5/11	The Spanish Suitcase
93	5/13	Forog
94	5/22	The Fireball of Milton Street
95	5/23	The Six Ingots of Leadenhall Street
96	5/24	Yehti

97	6/1	Seagoon MCC (original title 'The Man Who Won the War')
98	6/2	The Secret Escritoire
99	6/19	The Jet-Propelled Guided NAAFI
100	7/3	The Nadger Plague
101	7/7	The Great Bank Robbery
102	7/10	What's My Line?
103	7/11	The Telephone
104	7/14	Emperor of the Universe
105	7/25	The Histories of Pliny the Elder
106	8/15	The Thing on the Mountain
107	8/26	The Great Statue Debate

For full details of the 'VINTAGE GOONS' series, see the Chronological Index, p., 11

RE-ISSUES: 'PICK OF THE GOONS'
Listed numerically as issued, with series/number references (V=Vintage Goons).
The CN numbers apply to each series; the whole series is ordered at a time.

First series—CN 267

1	5/1	The Whistling Spy Enigma
2	5/5	The Affair of the Lone Banana
3	6/4	Napoleon's Piano
4	V/1	The Mummified Priest
5	6/26	Scradje
6	6/6	Rommel's Treasure
7	6/8	Shangri-La Again
8	V/14	The Albert Memorial
9	V/2	The Greatest Mountain in the World
10	V/6	The Vanishing Room
11	V/9	The Internal Mountain
12	V/11	The Great Bank of England Robbery
13	6/27	The Man Who Never Was
14	7/9	The Case of the Fake Neddie Seagoons (original title 'The Mystery of the Fake Neddie Seagoons')
15	7/12	The Flea
16	7/18	The Moon Show
17	7/19	The Mysterious Punch-up-the-Conker
18	7/20	Round the World in Eighty Days
19	7/21	Insurance, the White Man's Burden
20	7/23	Ill Met by Goonlight
21	8/4	The Great Regent's Park Swim
22	8/9	The Policy
23	9/5	The Mountain Eaters
24	9/8	Queen Anne's Rain
25	9/12	The Call of the West
26	9/16	The Gold Plate Robbery

Second series—CN 756

27	5/2	The Lost Gold Mine
28	5/6	The Canal
29	5/8	The Mystery of the Marie Celeste — Solved
30	5/16	The Case of the Missing Heir
31	5/19	The Missing Scroll
32	5/21	The Sinking of Westminster Pier
33	5/26	Confessions of a Secret Senna-pod Drinker (original title 'The End')
34	6/10	The Pevensey Bay Disaster
35	6/11	The Lost Colony (original title 'The Sale of Manhattan')

36	6/18	Tales of Montmartre
37	6/22	The Choking Horror
38	6/24	The Treasure in the Lake
39	7/5	The Spectre of Tintagel
40	7/8	Personal Narrative
41	7/15	Wings Over Dagenham
42	7/17	Shifting Sands
43	7/22	The Africa Ship Canal
44	7/24	The Missing Boa Constrictor
45	8/6	The Space Age
46	8/5	The Treasure in the Tower
47	8/11	The Stolen Postman
48	8/12	The Great British Revolution
49	8/3	The Burning Embassy
50	8/20	Ten Snowballs that Shook the World
51	8/18	The Curse of Frankenstein
52	8/22	'_____!' (original title 'World War One')
53	8/23	The Spon Plague
54	9/2	I Was Monty's Treble
55	9/7	The Seagoon Memoirs
56	10/4	Robin's Post
57	10/6	The Last Smoking Seagoon
58	10/1	A Christmas Carol

Third series—CN 1546/SS
59	5/4	The Phantom Head Shaver
60*	5/25	The White Box of Great Bardfield
61	5/18	Under Two Floorboards
62*	6/3	The Lost Emperor
63	6/5	The Case of the Missing CD Plates
64	7/6	The Sleeping Prince
65	6/9	The International Christmas Pudding
66*	6/14	The Greenslade Story
67	6/20	The House of Teeth
68	6/23	The Great Tuscan Salami Scandal
69*	6/25	The Fear of Wages
70*	7/1	The Nasty Affair at the Burami Oasis
71	7/2	Drums along the Mersey

Fourth series—CN 1645/SS
72*	6/7	Foiled by President Fred
73*	7/16	The Rent Collector (original title 'The Rent Collectors')
74	V/4	The Giant Bombardon
75	8/10	King Solomon's Mines
76	8/13	The Plasticine Man
77	8/17	The Moriarty Murder Mystery
78	8/16	The String Robberies
79	V/10	The Silent Bugler
80*	9/1	The Sahara Desert Statue
81	9/3	The £1,000,000 Penny
82	9/6	The Childe Harolde Rewarde
83	10/5	The Silver Dubloons
84	Special	Robin Hood

* not previously issued by Transcription Services

Listed chronologically with series/number reference.
Prefixes: T=tape. LP=pressed long play record. MT=tape from acetate original. No prefix=78 rpm disc. X or MX=33$\frac{1}{3}$ rpm coarse groove 16″ disc.
Some versions are as edited for Transcription Services (and are in fact LPs pressed from stampers for the original TS issues); these are indicated.

MT 20354	4/23	The Greatest Mountain in the World (originally X 20354-5)
T 28575	5/1	The Whistling Spy Enigma
T 28576	5/3	The Dreaded Batter-Pudding Hurler (of Bexhill-on-Sea)
T 28577	5/7	Lurgi Strikes Britain
T 28578	5/8	The Mystery of the Marie Celeste (Solved)
T 28579	5/9	The Last Tram (from Clapham)
T 28580	5/11	The Spanish Suitcase
T 28581	5/14	Ye Bandit of Sherwood Forest
T 22011	5/17	China Story (originally X 22011-12)
T 22011	5/18	Under Two Floorboards (originally X 22011-12)
T 28582	5/21	The Sinking of Westminster Pier
T 28583	5/24	Yehti
T 28584	5/25	The White Box of Great Bardfield
T 28585	6/7	Foiled by President Fred
T 28586	6/14	The Greenslade Story
T 28587	6/18	Tales of Montmartre
T 28588	6/19	The Jet-Propelled Guided NAAFI
T 28589	6/21	Tales of Old Dartmoor
LP 22776	6/23	The Great Tuscan Salami Scandal
T 28590	7/4	The MacReekie Rising of '74
T 28591	7/7	The Great Bank Robbery
T 28592	7/9	The Mystery of the Fake Neddie Seagoons
T 28593	SP	Robin Hood
T 32818	7/17	Shifting Sands
LP 27269	7/21	Insurance, the White Man's Burden (TS version)
LP 27274	7/23	Ill Met by Goonlight (TS version)
T 28594	7/25	The Histories of Pliny the Elder
LP 27276	8/16	The String Robberies (TS version)
LP 24017	8/19	The White Neddie Trade
T 28596	8/21	The Man Who Never Was
LP 27268	8/23	The Spon Plague (TS version)
LP 27270	9/2	I Was Monty's Treble (TS version)
LP 27271	9/5	The Mountain Eaters (TS version)
LP 27272	9/7	The Seagoon Memoirs (TS version)
LP 27273	9/8	Queen Anne's Rain (TS version)
LP 27275	9/13	Dishonoured—Again (TS version)
LP 27277	9/14	The Scarlet Capsule (TS version)
LP 25747	9/16	The Gold Plate Robbery
LP 27278	10/1	A Christmas Carol (TS version)
LP 26002	10/2	The Tale of Men's Shirts
LP 27278	10/6	The Last Smoking Seagoon (TS version)

The following are also in Sound Archives:

20529	4/13	*excerpt* from 'The Giant Bombardon' 2′17″
LP 25694		The Starlings
T 28595		The Reason Why
T 30055		The GPO Show
T 34807		The Last Goon Show of All

4: OTHER BROADCASTS BY THE GOONS

It would be quite impossible in the space available to list all individual appearances by the four Goons. In order to qualify for inclusion, a broadcast must include two or more Goons; reminiscences and interviews of a more serious nature have not been listed, but mainly entertainment programmes. The entries are in chronological order. Mention should be made of 'Listen, My Children', which, although it does not qualify for listing here as only Secombe appears in it, was one of the programmes that paved the way for 'The Goon Show'. The series ran for eight shows between June 1 and July 20, 1948, in the Home Service; it was produced by Pat Dixon.

'ROOFTOP RENDEZVOUS'

Cabaret-type programme; those appearing included Harry Secombe (a troublesome guest) and Michael Bentine (just troublesome). Also appearing: Billy Reid and Dorothy Squires, Jack Billings, Stanelli, Peter Brough & Archie Andrews, Gaston Palmer, Audrey Wayne, Michael Moore, Laurie Watson, The Rooftop Lovelies, and Jack Jackson with the Rendezvous Orchestra. Devised and produced by Richard Afton. BBC-Television, 2100-2200 approx., 1-1-49.

'THIRD DIVISION — some vulgar fractions'

with Robert Beatty, Benny Lee, Bruce Belfrage, Patricia Hayes, Harry Secombe, Peter Sellers (except 16-2-49), Michael Bentine, Benny Hill, Carole Carr, Margaret Lindsay, Robert Moreton, The George Mitchell Choir, and Vic Lewis and his Orchestra (strings under Reginald Leopold).
Scripts by Frank Muir and Denis Norden. Additional material by Paul Dehn. Produced by Pat Dixon.
Broadcast Third Programme, Wednesdays; times below are as shown in *Radio Times* but, in the case of Third Programme, these were usually pretty nominal.

1	26-1-49	2000-2035	SOX 15355	(recorded 6-12-48)
2	2-2-49	2020-2050	SLO 43204	(recorded 8-12-48)
3	9-2-49	2000-2030	SLO 43000	(recorded 11-12-48)
4	16-2-49	2000-2030	SLO 43421	(recorded 16-12-48)
5	23-2-49	2055-2125	SAL 15423	(recorded 18-12-48)
6	2-3-49	2000-2035	SLO 43747	(recorded 29-12-48)

This series was a follow-up to 'Listen, My Children'. 'Third Division' was referred to (though not by name) in the *Radio Times* publicity at the beginning of the 5th series of the Goon Show as a 'super-intellectual advanced comedy show' giving the first outlet to Goonism. This is not quite an accurate description of the show's style, which was more restrained than 'The Goon Show'. Unfortunately no recordings have survived. The original recordings detailed above were $33^1/_3$ r.p.m. coarse groove 16" disks recorded (over landline from the studio) at Broadcasting House (SLO), 200 Oxford Street (SOX) or Aldenham House (SAL).

'BUMBLETHORPE' — 2nd of series

with Robert Moreton, Avril Angers, Peter Sellers (replacing Valentine Dyall at short notice), Kenneth Connor, Graham Stark, Spike Milligan, Denise Bryer, Alfred Marks and Robin Richmond at the Hammond Organ. The Dance Orchestra conducted by Stanley Black. Script by Spike Milligan, Larry Stephens and Peter Ling. Produced by Peter Eton.
Broadcast 19-11-51 in the Home Service, 1945-2015; recorded earlier the same day on SLO 98472.

'TRIAL GALLOP'

Michael Bentine, Peter Sellers, Leslie Mitchell, Leslie Randall, Peter Butterworth, Graham Stark, Jack Hayes, John Vivienne, Clementina Stuart, and Anne Hayes.
This was the first of several attempts to transmit the Goons on television. Scheduled for broadcast on BBC Television from 2055 to 2140 on February 13, 1952, it was cancelled owing to the death of King George VI.

As it was to have been 'live', re-scheduling it was not possible without re-booking all the artists, and in the end the Goons were seen on television screens in a somewhat different form:

'GOONREEL — a television newsreel'
Commentator Andrew Timothy; with Michael Bentine, Peter Sellers, Spike Milligan, Eunice Grayson, Graham Stark, Sam Kydd, Robert Cawdron, Clementina Stuart, Jack Hayes, Leslie Crowther, Valentine Prorovitch, Allan Gabriel, Margaret Lawford; and Harry Secombe (on film). Script by Michael Bentine, Jimmy Grafton and Spike Milligan. Music and special orchestrations by Jack Jordan; orchestra directed by Eric Robinson. Devised, presented, directed and produced by Mr. Claude Boote, assisted by Michael Mills. Broadcast on BBC-TV, 2045-2130, 2-7-52.

'DON'T SPARE THE HORSES'
From the Princess Theatre, London. With Jimmy James, Hutton Connors, Dick Carlton, Erroll Stephens, John Hanson, Clifford Stanton, The Three Monarchs, Peter Sellers, Spike Milligan, Tutte Lemkow, Sarah Luzita, David Croft, Wilfred Johns, John Orchard; Lyrics and Script by Jimmy Grafton. Music by Cyril Ornandel and Jack Jordan. Produced by W. Lyon-Shaw. Broadcast on BBC-TV, 2120-2220, 1-11-52.

'THE HUNDREDTH BOAT RACE — in which Jimmy Edwards and Dick Bentley become involved in Boat Race Day on the towpath'
Also with Arthur Askey, Valentine Dyall, Arthur English, Joyce Grenfell, A. E. Matthews, Spike Milligan, Harry Secombe, Peter Sellers, John Snagge, Terry-Thomas, Ralph Wightman, Jack Hawkins, Rudolf Offenbach, Noel Johnson and Frank Marchant. Written and produced by John Bridges. Broadcast live in Home Service, 1945-2030, 2-4-54; Askey, English and Matthews pre-recorded their contributions.

'THE LID OFF THE BBC — No. 4; The Variety Department'
One of a series of behind-the-scenes documentaries about the BBC, this programme took a special look at the Goons. With Spike Milligan, Harry Secombe, Peter Sellers, Dick Katz, Ray Ellington, Frank Muir and Denis Norden. (Dick Katz was the pianist in the Ray Ellington Quartet of the period.) With a recorded extract from 'The End' (last of 5th series). The programme was written and narrated by Wilfred Thomas, and produced by Alan Burgess. Broadcast in the Home Service, 1930-2000 on 4-5-55; pre-recorded 3-5-55 on TLO 78716.

'SECOMBE HERE!' — 1st of an occasional series of three
Harry Secombe with Shirley Eaton, Spike Milligan, Maria Pavlou, Valentine Dyall, Eric Sykes, Clifford Stanton, Paulette and Rona, John Vyvyan, Victor Platt, Peter Glover, Katherine Feather, The Peter Glover Dancers and The George Mitchell Singers. Script by Jimmy Grafton, Spike Milligan and Eric Sykes. Produced by W. Lyon-Shaw. Broadcast on BBC-TV, 2131-2230, 14-5-55.

'SECOMBE HERE!' — 3rd of series
Harry Secombe with Peter Sellers, Ruby Murray, Ted and George Durante, Audrey Jeans, The Three Arnauts, Libby Morris, Sam Kydd, John Vyvyan, Peter Glover, The Peter Glover Dancers, The George Mitchell Singers. Produced by Albert Stevenson. Broadcast live from the Radio Show at Earl's Court, BBC-TV, 2045-2145, 3-9-55.
The following programme, 'O.B.Parade', also live from Earl's Court, ended with Spike Milligan and Eric Sykes doing the 'stick dance' with Harry Secombe (who was not billed and appears simply not to have gone home after his own programme).

'THE LISTENING ROOM'
Peter Sellers with some records in 'The Listening Room'. (The Critics: Hercules Grytpype-Thynne; Major Dennis Bloodnok; Mr. Henry Crun; John Britanearly; a small boy.) Spike Milligan appeared briefly on pre-recorded inserts; the programme

144

also included 'I'm Walking Backwards for Christmas' (BBC recording) and 'Dance With Me, Henry' (unissued Parlophone recording). Produced by Michael Bell. Broadcast live in the Light Programme, 1930-2000, 28-12-55.

'THE IDIOT WEEKLY PRICE 2d'
Two programmes under this title were broadcast by Associated-Rediffusion Television on February 24 and April 6, 1956, both 2200 to 2230. 'Idiot Weekly' was a Victorian-type newspaper, of which Peter Sellers was the Editor. Graham Stark, Valentine Dyall, Kenneth Connor, Patti Lewis, and Spike Milligan featured in both shows, with the addition of Eric Sykes and June Whitfield in the first show and Max Geldray in the second. Both shows were directed by Dick Lester, whilst the script-credit for the first show read: 'Scripts provided by Associated London Scripts, edited by Eric Sykes with contributions by Spike Milligan'.

'A SHOW CALLED FRED'
Peter Sellers, with Spike Milligan, and a well-known cast of Thespians and Actors, including Valentine Dyall, Kenneth Connor, Graham Stark, Patti Lewis, and Max Geldray. Directed by Dick Lester. Broadcast on Associated-Rediffusion Television, Wednesdays, 2130-2200.

1	2-5-56	3	16-5-56	5	30-5-56
2	9-5-56	4	23-5-56		

'SON OF FRED'
Peter Sellers and Spike Milligan, with Valentine Dyall, Kenneth Connor, Graham Stark, Patti Lewis, Max Geldray, and Johnny Vyvyan, with additional cast as shown below:

CH=Cuthbert Harding   MF=Mario Fabrizi
JL=Jennifer Lautrec   ES=Eric Sykes
 TA=The Alberts (these artists appear by arrangement with money)

Music by the Reg Owen Orchestra. Animated Cartoons by Biographic. Directed by Dick Lester. Broadcast by Associated-Rediffusion Television and regional companies on Mondays, 2130-2200.

1	17- 9-56	CH
2	24- 9-56	CH
3	1-10-56	CH, MF, JL
4	8-10-56	CH, MF, JL, TA
5	15-10-56	CH, MF, JL, TA, ES
6	22-10-56	CH, MF, JL, TA
7	29-10-56	CH, MF, JL, TA
8	5-11-56	MF, JL

'OFF THE RECORD—Jack Payne introduces stars and personalities who are "Off the Record"'
The programme included Spike Milligan and Peter Sellers, miming to 'The Ying Tong Song'. Broadcast on BBC-TV, 2130-2200, 10-12-56.

'YES, IT'S THE CATHODE RAY TUBE SHOW'
Peter Sellers, Michael Bentine, and David Nettheim. Scripts by Michael Bentine and David Nattheim. Music by Steve Race and his orchestra. Produced and directed by Kenneth Carter. Associated-Rediffusion Television, Mondays, 2130-2200.

1	11-2-57	3	25-2-57	5	11-3-57
2	18-2-57	4	4-3-57	6	18-3-57

'THE TELEGOONS' — first series
Eleven of the original Goon Show scripts were shortened and re-worked by Maurice Wiltshire, to provide the basis for this series of fifteen-minute puppet films. The puppets were designed by Ralph Young, father of Tony Young of Grosvenor Films, who made the programmes for the BBC. Broadcast on BBC-TV at 1740 on Saturdays.

1	5-10-63	The Ascent of Mount Everest
2	12-10-63	The Lost Colony
3	19-10-63	The Fear of Wages
4	26-10-63	Napoleon's Piano
5	2-11-63	The Last Tram
	9-11-63	(No broadcast owing to the Festival of Remembrance)
6	16-11-63	China Story
7	23-11-63	The Canal
	30-11-63	('The Choking Horror' was scheduled, but was postponed to allow the first episode of a new serial called 'Doctor Who' to be repeated immediately prior to the second episode.)
9	7-12-63	The Hastings Flyer
10	14-12-63	The Mystery of the Marie Celeste — Solved!
11	21-12-63	The International Christmas Pudding
8	28-12-63	The Choking Horror

'THE TELEGOONS' — 2nd series
A further fifteen programmes were produced in the same way. They were broadcast on BBC-1 TV on Saturdays, at 1715 (nos. 1-6), 1700 (7-12, 15 & 13) and 1725 (no. 14).

1	28- 3-64	Scradje
2	4- 4-64	The Booted Gorilla
3	11- 4-64	The Underwater Mountain (original title 'The Greatest Mountain in the World')
4	18- 4-64	The Dreaded Batter-Pudding Hurler of Bexhill-on-Sea
5	25- 4-64	Tales of Old Dartmoor
6	2- 5-64	Lurgi Strikes Britain
7	9- 5-64	Captain Seagoon R.N. (original title 'Personal Narrative')
8	16- 5-64	The First Albert Memorial to the Moon
9	23- 5-64	The Whistling Spy Enigma
10	30- 5-64	Tales of Montmartre
11	6- 6-64	The Africa Ship Canal
12	13- 6-64	The Affair of the Lone Banana
	20- 6-64	('The Terrible Revenge of Fred Fu-Manchu' was scheduled, but postponed to make way for cricket from Lord's)
14	27- 6-64	The Nadger Plague
	4- 7-64	
	11- 7-64	(Not scheduled, to allow extension of 'Summer Grandstand')
15	18- 7-64	The Siege of Fort Knight
	25- 7-64	('Summer Grandstand')
13	1- 8-64	The Terrible Revenge of Fred Fu-Manchu

The series was immediately followed by repeats of six of the first series; BBC-TV, Saturdays at 1700 (first two), 1715 (next three), and 1745.

5	8- 8-64	The Last Tram
6	15- 8-64	China Story
7	22- 8-64	The Canal
	29- 8-64	('Summer Grandstand')
8	5- 9-64	The Choking Horror
9	12- 9-64	The Hastings Flyer
10	19- 9-64	The Mystery of the Marie Celeste — Solved!

146

'FORCES GALA NIGHT'
A special programme to celebrate the 21st anniversary of the British Forces Broadcasting Service. The Goons contributed a shortened version of 'I Was Monty's Treble'. Harry Secombe, Spike Milligan, and David Jacobs as the announcer were at the recording session in London on 1-11-64, together with the other artists contributing, and Cliff Michelmore, the compère; Peter Sellers contributed via a land-line from Paris. The duration of the Goon item was 7'45". Broadcast 1800-1930 in the Light Programme, 8-11-64; the BBC General Overseas Service joined for the last hour, which included the Goons. Recording number TLO 51295; recorded at the Victoria Palace.

'THE GRAND PIANO ORCHESTRA SHOW' ('THE G.P.O. SHOW')
Home Service, 1310-1340, 25-12-64. With Spike Milligan, Harry Secombe, John Bluthal, Barry Humphries, Garry Miller, Announcer; Bob Todd. The Grand Piano Orchestra, leader John Jezard, conducted by Paul Fenoulhet. Script: Spike Milligan. Producer: Charles Chilton. Recorded before the Postmaster-General and an audience of Post Office workers, 20-12-64, on TLO 54423. This partly comprises a re-working of the Goon Show script of 'The History of Communications' (29-1-54). It is one of a set of three shows, all broadcast at holiday times, the others being 'The Army Show' (16-6-65) and the 'Naughty Navy Show' (25-12-65). It was originally staged for Post Office personnel, but with the sort of luck which bedevilled many true Goon Shows, the Post Office objected to the title 'The G.P.O. Show' on the grounds that the initials G.P.O. were a registered trade-mark, so the title was hastily changed to 'The Grand Piano Orchestra Show'.

'SECOMBE AND FRIENDS'
Part of this programme was the result of an attempt by Associated-Rediffusion to stage a Goon Show. A set simulating a BBC radio studio was constructed, and the cast performed at a microphone in the manner of a radio broadcast, in front of an invited audience. The proceedings were video recorded. However the complete show was considered too uninteresting visually, and in 'Secombe and Friends' Secombe and Ellington reminisced and introduced excerpts from the video tape, only about half of which was seen by the viewers. The Goon Show chosen was 'The Whistling Spy Enigma'; the duration of this part of the programme (minus adverts.) was 17'15". Broadcast 1830-1930, 16-10-66, Associated-Rediffusion Television and regional companies.

'THE GOON SHOW — TALES OF MEN'S SHIRTS'
Peter Sellers, Harry Secombe, Spike Milligan, with John Cleese as the announcer. Produced by Peter Eton. Again, this was in effect a televised radio production. Duration (without adverts) 23'20". Broadcast by Thames Television and regional companies, 2000-2030. 8-8-68.

THE LAST GOON SHOW OF ALL'
Peter Sellers, Spike Milligan, Harry Secombe, Ray Ellington, Max Geldray, Orchestra conducted by Peter Knight. Script by Spike Milligan. Produced by John Browell. Recorded at the Camden Theatre, Sunday 30th April 1972; the mono recording made by Broadcasting House on TLN/18/LH343 was edited to 46'10" including playout and broadcast on BBC Radio 4, 2000-2045, 5-10-72, as part of the BBC's 50th Anniversary celebrations. This recording was subsequently placed in Sound Archives. BBC Transcription Services made their own stereo recording, which they issued, and which has also been issued to the public on LP (see appendix 5, no. 14). The proceedings were also video taped and broadcast on BBC-1 on 26-12-72.

PARKINSON MEETS THE GOONS'
This was one of a regular series of 'chat shows' chaired by Michael Parkinson. Sellers and Secombe were in the studio; Milligan, who was ill in bed in Australia, participated on filmed inserts. Music was provided by the Ray Ellington Quartet.

147

Broadcast on BBC-1 at 2315 on 28-10-72; duration 1 hour 13$^1/_2$ minutes. A shortened version was subsequently issued on LP (see appendix 5, no. 15).

'SING A SONG OF SECOMBE'
Broadcast on BBC-1, 1925 to 2015, 29-12-74.
Starring Harry Secombe, with his special guests Peter Sellers, Spike Milligan, Nina, The Nolans, and Aiden J. Harvey. with Peter Knight and his Orchestra. Written by Jimmy Grafton and Peter Vincent. Additional material by Spike Mullins and John Muir. Director Stanley Appel; producer Stewart Morris. The other two Goons joined Secombe for a short sequence at the end of the show, firstly in a filmed insert of the three masquerading as buskers in London's Oxford Street (with Milligan giving a rare demonstration of his trumpet-playing ability), and then, on a video taped insert, as 'The Brothers MacGoonigal' reading 'The Famous Tay Whale' by William McGonagall. Duration of sequence 6'23".

5: COMMERCIAL RECORDS OF GOON MATERIAL

In compiling this discography, it has been difficult to define what constitutes 'Goon Material'. Sellers, Secombe, Milligan, Bentine, Geldray and Ellington have all made records on their own, but most of these are clearly outside the scope of a Goonography. Here, only records which feature two or more of the artists, or records which specifically claim to be Goon records in the title or on the label, are listed.

* indicates that the record has been deleted from the catalogue and is no longer available.

10-inch 78 r.p.m. records
1. ***DECCA F.10756**
    The Bluebottle Blues (with Maurice Ponke and his Orchestre Fromage)
    I'm Walking Backwards for Christmas (with Nick Rauchen conducting the Ball's Pond Road near 'The One-in-Harmony')
    Recorded early May 1956, published August 1956

2. ***DECCA F.10780**
    Bloodnok's Rock'n'Roll Call (featuring Major Dennis Bloodnok, 43rd Deserters [Rtd.], with Roland Rockcake and his Wholly Rollers)
    The Ying Tong Song (with Maurice Ponke and his Orchestre Fromage)
    Recorded August 1956, published October 1956

3. ***PARLOPHONE R.4251**
    My September Love (The Famous ECCLES and Miss Freda Thing, with Mr. Reginald Owen and his excruciating orchestra)
    You Gotta Go OWW! (Count Jim Moriarty, with Gravely Stephens (Pharmacological Pianist) and the Massed Alberts)
    Recorded early September 1956, published December 1956; with Milligan and Eric Sykes only

4. ***DECCA F.10885**
    Eeh! Ah! Oh! Ooh! (with Orchestra conducted by Sir)
    I Love You (featuring Slim Idiot and the Sons of the Bicycle Saddle)
    Published May 1957

5. ***DECCA F.10945**
    Whistle Your Cares Away (featuring Whistler's Mother-in-Law and Asian Flu [duetists])
    A Russian Love Song (with Igor Blimey and his Romanoff Café Fred Players. Featuring Zym Balist on his Collective Farm). Published November 1957

7-inch 45 r.p.m. singles
Nos. 1, 2, 4, & 5 above were issued in this form under the same catalogue numbers but with the prefix '45 —'; these are all now deleted. 'The Ying Tong Song' and 'I'm Walking Backwards for Christmas' were re-issued on Decca F.13414 in 1973; it entered the Top Twenty on 4-8-73, and spent five weeks in the charts, reaching as high as no. 9.

7-inch 45 r.p.m. E.P.s
Nos. 1 & 2 above were issued on Decca *DFE.6396 in October 1957 under the title 'The Goons'.

6. ***PARLOPHONE GEP.8764: 'GOON WITH THE WIND'** (Max Geldray)
    Once in Love with Amy; Crazy Rhythm; It's Only a Paper Moon: Our Love is Here to Stay; Chérie; Duke's Joke.
    Studio recordings, not from Goon Shows. Published September 1959.

10-inch 33¹/₃ r.p.m. L.P.
Nos. 1, 2, 4 & 5 above were issued on Decca *LF.1332 in September 1964 under the title 'Unchained Melodies'.

12-inch 33^1/$_3$ r.p.m. L.P.s

7. PARLOPHONE PMC. 1108: 'BEST OF THE GOON SHOWS'
Tales of Old Dartmoor (from the broadcast of 7-2-56)
Dishonoured (correctly titled 'Dishonoured — Again'; broadcast 26-1-59)
Both shows are somewhat shortened, with both musical spots deleted and the
closing signature tune faded early. Published October 1959. Also issued on 3^3/$_4$
i.p.s. 8-track cartridge, Parlophone 8X-PCS.1108; and on Musicassette,
Parlophone TC-PCS.1108 (Dolby).

8. PARLOPHONE PMC.1129: 'BEST OF THE GOON SHOWS No. 2'
Tales of Men's Shirts (broadcast 31-12-59)
The Scarlet Capsule (broadcast 2-2-59)
Both shows are somewhat shortened, with both musical spots deleted and the
closing signature tune faded early. Published late 1960.

9. *PARLOPHONE PMC.1190: 'THE BRIDGE ON THE RIVER WYE' (Stereo
version PCS.3036) with Sellers, Milligan, Jonathan Miller, Peter Cook, Peter
Rawley, Patricia Ridgway, and orchestra conducted by Wally Stott. Based in
part upon 'African Incident' (8/14). Published November 1962.

10. PARLOPHONE PMC.7037: 'GOON BUT NOT FORGOTTEN'
Six Charlies in Search of an Author (broadcast 26-12-56)
Insurance — the White Man's Burden (broadcast 28-2-57)
Again, both musical spots have been deleted. Published November 1967.
Also issued on 3^3/$_4$ i.p.s. open reel tape record, Parlophone *TA-PMC.7037.

11. PARLOPHONE PMC.7062: 'GOON AGAIN'
China Story (broadcast 18-1-55)
The MacReekie Rising of '74 (broadcast 25-10-56).
Both musical spots have been deleted. Spike Milligan is not present on 'The
MacReekie Rising of '74', despite what it says on the record sleeve. Published
October 1968.

12. PARLOPHONE PMC.7132: 'FIRST MEN ON THE GOON'
Foiled by President Fred (broadcast 1-11-55)
Robin Hood and his Merry Men (recorded 2-12-56, not broadcast in U.K.)
Both musical spots have been deleted. In the case of 'Foiled by President Fred',
several musical links and the 'Harry Lime Theme' (sung by Bluebottle) have
also been cut. Published October 1971.

13. *PHILIPS AL.3464: 'HOW TO WIN AN ELECTION (or not lose by much)'
What it's all about; Man to man; Left a little; Man of the people; Worst of both
worlds: Keep right on; To Home it may concern; West side Tory; On Her
Majesty's Swinging Service; It's the man that counts.
Peter Sellers, Harry Secombe, and Spike Milligan. Written and devised by
Leslie Bricusse. Sellers's contribution was recorded in Hollywood and edited in.
Published April 1964.

14. BBC RECORDS REB.142S (stereo): 'THE LAST GOON SHOW OF ALL'
Recorded 30-4-72. Stereo recording by BBC Transcription Services; the
recording is as edited for the Transcription Services issue; the BBC Records
issue is in fact pressed from the same stampers. Published October 1972. Also
issued on 8-track cartridge, BBC Records RCT.8000, and on musicassette,
BBC Records REMC.142.

15. **BBC RECORDS REB.165M (mono): 'PARKINSON MEETS THE GOONS'**
Slightly shortened soundtrack of the broadcast on BBC-TV, 28-10-72.
Published October 1973.

16. **BBC RECORDS REC.172 (stereo): 'GOON SHOW HITS'** (The Ray Ellington Quartet)
Framed; The Three Bears; I've Got a Girl in Kalamazoo; Signora; Buona Sera; The Lady's in Love with You; Little Girl; That's My Girl; The Teddy Bears' Picnic; Old Man River; Old Mother Hubbard; My very good Friend the Milkman; It's a Sin to Tell a Lie; I want a Little Girl; From This Moment On. These are BBC studio recordings, not from Goon Shows. Published March 1974.

17. **BBC RECORDS REB.177 (mono): 'GOON SHOW CLASSICS'**
The Dreaded Batter-Pudding Hurler (broadcast 12-10-54)
The Histories of Pliny the Elder (broadcast 28-3-57)
These are the uncut transmission versions, with both musical spots intact. Published September 1974. Also issued on 8-track cartridge, BBC Records RCT.8009; and on musicassette, BBC Records RMC.4010.

18. **E.M.I. EMC.3062 ('stereo'): 'THE VERY BEST OF THE GOONS — 1.'**
The Missing Ten Downing Street (recorded 3-11-57; not broadcast in U.K.)
The Red Fort (broadcast 11-11-57)
Both musical spots deleted. 'Electronically processed for stereo effect', i.e., slight 'spread' and unpleasant bathroom-type acoustic added, which only succeeds in spoiling the atmosphere so carefully created by the Goons and the production staff. Published December 1974. Also issued on 8-track cartridge, E.M.I. 8X-EMC.3062; and on musicassette, E.M.I. TC-EMC.3062 (Dolby).

19. **DECCA SKL.5194 (stereo): 'HE'S INNOCENT OF WATERGATE'**
Star Spangled Banner; Opening Announcement; The Notorious Missing Tape — Found; The President Works Late; The President Meets the Guardian of the Tapes; The White House Intruder; Phone Call to Duke Ellington; The Rehearsal; At Prayer: The Misfit; Detente with China; A Meeting of Presidents; Britain for Ever; In the Bunker; The End.
Peter Sellers and Spike Milligan with Sandra Caron, John Bluthal, Bill Mitchell, Ed Bishop & June Whitfield. Script by Spike Milligan, Alan Coren, N. F. Simpson, John Bird, Barry Took, Richard Ingrams & Barry Fantoni. Published late 1974.

20. **BBC RECORDS REB.213 (mono): 'GOON SHOW CLASSICS No. 2'**
The Jet-Propelled Guided NAAFI (broadcast 24-1-56)
The Evils of Bushey Spon (broadcast 17-3-58)
Both shows are complete with the musical items; 'NAAFI' is the original Transcription Services version; 'Bushey Spon' is complete as originally broadcast except for two tiny cuts. For those puzzled by music credits on the sleeve to Angela Morley, it should be pointed out that Angela Morley *was* Wally Stott. Published October 1975; also issued on 8-track cartridge, BBC Records RCT.8007; and on musicassette, BBC Records RMC.4026.

6: MISCELLANEOUS GOON MATERIAL

1. 'UNCHAINED MELODY'

Bluebottle and Eccles's rendering of this hit song of 1955 was recorded by Parlophone that year but never issued because the publishers of the original objected strenuously to this parody. It was partly as a result of the bad feeling arising out of this that the Goons moved to Decca the following year (see Appendix 5). A few copies of this recording have escaped and are in private hands. Duration 2′48″.

2. 'DANCE WITH ME, HENRY'

Presumably intended as the reverse side of 'Unchained Melody', this item surfaced briefly in 'The Listening Room', Light Programme 28-12-55 (see Appendix 4), in the Programmes as Broadcast details for which it was identified as 'Parlophone (unissued)'. Unfortunately no copies of this seem to have survived, although possibly Parlophone still have the tapes. Duration 1′07″ broadcast (although this may have been only an excerpt).

3. EFFECTS FOR 'THE GOON SHOW'

In 1962 the BBC Sound-Effects Department, which is responsible for the huge library of sound effects available on pressed 78s and LPs for use within the BBC, issued two 12-inch vinyl 78s from surviving Goon Show effects tapes. The contents are listed below; some of the sounds will be familiar to Goon fans, although others (such as the cod duck and the milk bottle breaking) do not seem to come from any Goon show and are in fact not particularly funny.

19 G 22   Front:
1.   Clock-type mechanism — 30″
2-3. Whoosh — 1″ each
4-5. Double whoosh — 2″, 3″
6-7. Coin dropped — 5″, 3″
8.   Several men coughing — 7″
9.   Wild hammering — 23″
10.   Crash with knives and forks — 7″
11.   Crash with ball-bearings — 5″

Back:
1. Footsteps down 9 flights of stairs — 1′12″
2. Wooden door wrecked — 53″
3. Cod duck — 12″
4. Pouring liquid; continuous — 40″

19 G 23   Front:
1-2. Crash beginning with bucket — 15″, 9″
3.   Spasmodic snoring — 33″
4.   Crowd panic — 20″
5-6. Piano crash — 20″ each
7.   Milk bottle breaking — 2″
8.   Three glass crashes — 11″

Back:
1. Red Indian battle — 32″
2. Storm at sea — 53″
3. Air raid — 17″
4. Veteran veteran car — 40″

The BBC Sound-Effects Department has also released, rather more recently, a series of about a dozen $33^1/_3$ r.p.m. 7-inch 'Comedy Effects' records (numbered EC.7A, EC.7B, etc) Some of these contain Goon effects, although not attributed as such. In particular, the famous Radiophonics Workshop piece 'Bloodnok's Stomach' appears on EC.7K, back, band 2 (8 seconds). It is always possible that as new discs are issued by the Sound Effects Centre more authentic Goon noises may appear. These records are not available to the public.

This list gives details of feature and short films in which two or more of the four original Goons appear, together with one which, though billed as a Goon film, stars only Sellers (although with Graham Stark and Ray Ellington). In general the films are rather poor compared with the Goon Shows; viewed from the Goon fan's point of view only *The Running, Jumping and Standing Still Film* and *The Case of the Mukkinese Battle Horn* are of other than curiosity interest.

FEATURE FILMS

The first feature film including three of the cast is not strictly speaking a Goon film, since it is not written by Milligan or any of the other Goon Show script-writers, but it is interesting as showing the main three members of the cast in their early days.

PENNY POINTS TO PARADISE
(Advance-PYL Productions [Adelphi] 1951)
Directed by Tony Young; Produced by Alan Cullimore
Screenplay by John Ormonde

Harry Flakers . . . . Harry Secombe
Edward Haynes . . . . Alfred Marks
The Major
Arnold P'Fringe   . . . . Peter Sellers
Spike Donnely . . . . Spike Milligan
Digger Graves . . . . Bill Kerr

with

Paddy O'Neil; Freddie Frinton; Vicki Page; Joe Linanne; Sam Kydd; and Felix Mendelssohn and his Hawaiian Serenaders
(77 minutes)

The film is more in the tradition of the British knockabout comedy than the Goon Show. Harry Flakers, having won £100,000 on the football pools, goes to stay with his friend Spike at a Brighton guest-house, where he attracts the attention of a couple of counterfeiters and a girl fortune-hunter. The counterfeiters steal Harry's money, substituting their own forged notes, and make off with the rest of the cast in pursuit. The chase culminates in a slapstick sequence in a waxworks museum.

The next feature film is an attempt to transfer the humour of the early Goon Shows to the screen, in which it is not entirely successful.

DOWN AMONG THE Z MEN
(New Realm, 1952)
Directed by Maclean Rogers; Produced by E. J. Fancey
Screenplay by Jimmy Grafton & Francis Charles

Professor Osric Pureheart . . . . . . Michael Bentine
Harry Jones . . . . Harry Secombe
Private Eccles . . . . Spike Milligan
Colonel Bloodnok . . . . Peter Sellers
Carole Gaylee . . . . Carole Carr
Spies . . . . Andrew Timothy
                            Graham Stark
W.R.A.C.s . . . . The Television Toppers

(71 minutes)

Harry Jones, grocer's assistant and amateur detective, follows Professor Pureheart, who has invented a secret atomic formula, to Warwell Atomic Research Station. In the Army camp attached to the station they get mixed up with some spies who are trying to steal the formula and a girl from M.I.5 who is trying to protect it. The film includes several song and dance numbers, plus a short demonstration of good jazz trumpet playing from Eccles. Notice that Bloodnok has been promoted to Colonel for this one appearance. He is, by comparison with the loose-bowelled old lecher of the late 1950s, almost a straight character. Eccles is also not quite as stupid as he becomes later. Bentine manages to perform his entire part with his eyes crossed; he also does his famous chair-back routine. The whole film is obviously hastily shot and assembled, and is rather messy. Parts of it are quite funny — not always the parts that were meant to be.

FORCES SWEETHEART
(New Realm, 1953)
Directed by Maclean Rogers; Produced by E. J. Fancey

Judy James	Hy Hazell
Harry Llewellen	Harry Secombe
John Robinson	Michael Bentine
Aloysius Dimwiddie	Freddie Frinton

with
John Ainsworth; Molly Weir; Adrian Scott; Graham Stark.
(76 minutes)

Three servicemen adopt the same name to woo a singer returned from entertaining the troops abroad. The film got very bad reviews at the time.

THE BED SITTING ROOM
(United Artists, 1969)
Directed and produced by Richard Lester
From the play by Spike Milligan & John Antrobus

Lord Fortnum	Ralph Richardson
Penelope	Rita Tushingham
Captain Bules Martin	Michael Hordern
Father	Arthur Lowe
Mother	Mona Washbourne
'Mate'	Spike Milligan
Shelter Man	Harry Secombe

with
Peter Cook, Dudley Moore, Roy Kinnear, Marty Feldman, Richard Warwick.
(91 minutes)

Milligan appears as a latter-day Willium, and Secombe as a sort of post-atomic Welsh Neddie Seagoon, in this highly surrealistic view of Britain after the Bomb.

Milligan makes a brief appearance in *The Magic Christian* (1969) which stars Sellers.

In *The Magnificent Seven Deadly Sins* (1971), Secombe appears in a sketch depicting Envy; Milligan appears in a separate sketch, personifying Sloth.

Milligan and Bentine appear, but do not work together, in *Rentadick* (1972).

Milligan appears as the Gryphon, and Sellers as the March Hare, in *Alice's Adventures in Wonderland* (1972) — again, they do not work together.

After this string of appearances in the same films but not together, two of the Goons at last work together in:

THE GREAT McGONAGALL
(Tigon, 1974)
Directed by Joseph McGrath
Produced by David Grant
Screenplay by Joseph McGrath & Spike Milligan
William J. McGonagall . . . . Spike Milligan
Queen Victoria . . . . Peter Sellers

with

John Bluthal, Valentine Dyall, Victor Spinetti, Julia Foster, Julian Chagrin, Clifton Jones, Charlie Atom and Janet Adair.
(89 minutes)

Unfortunately, the film was not a success and received uniformly bad reviews.

SHORT FILMS

LET'S GO CRAZY
(Advance Productions [Adelphi] , 1951)
Directed by Alan Cullimore

Groucho
Giuseppe
Cedric . . . . Peter Sellers
Izzy Gozzunk
Crystal Jollibottom

Eccles . . . . Spike Milligan

with

Wallas Eaton; Manly and Austin; and Freddie Mirfield's Garbage Men.
(32 minutes)

LONDON ENTERTAINS
(E. J. Fancey Productions, 1951)
Directed by E. J. Fancey
Screenplay by Jimmy Grafton

with

Eamonn Andrews; Christine Forrest; Pamela Bygraves; Vincent Ball; The Eastbourne Girls Choir; Bobby Breen; Paul Adam; Diana Coupland; Tony Fayne; David Evans; Peter Sellers; Harry Secombe; and Spike Milligan.
(48 minutes)

Some girls from a Swiss finishing school set up an escort agency; showing their clients around London, they visit, among other places, a BBC studio to see 'The Goon Show' in action.

THE SUPER SECRET SERVICE
(New Realm, 1953)
Directed by Charles W. Green
Screenplay by Spike Milligan

with
Peter Sellers; Graham Stark; Dick Emery; and the
Ray Ellington Quartet.
(26 minutes)

Although billed in the publicity as being 'the Radio Goon Show boys' idea of M.I.5'
only one of the main three is present, although the others appeared in some shows and
Milligan wrote the screenplay, which once again involves secret formulae and M.I.5.

THE CASE OF THE MUKKINESE BATTLE HORN (1956)
Directed by Joseph Sterling
Story by Larry Stephens
Screenplay by Harry Booth, John Penington,
and Larry Stephens.
starring
Peter Sellers, Spike Milligan and Dick Emery
with
Pamela Thomas, Bill Hepper, Wally Thomas,
and Gordon Phillot.
(29 minutes)

The theft from a museum of a rare old 9th-century Mukkinese Battle-Horn is being
investigated by Inspector Quilt (Sellers) and Sergeant Brown (Milligan). They cross-
examine the curator of the museum, Nodule (Emery); Eccles, and Henry Crun,
proprietor of a pawn shop. Eventually they trace the theft to a gang of International
Mukkinese Battle-Horn smugglers, headed by Nodule.
Filmed in the wonder of Schizophrenoscope (the new Split Screen).

THE RUNNING, JUMPING AND STANDING STILL FILM
(Produced by Peter Sellers Productions 1959)
Directed by Richard Lester

with
Peter Sellers, Spike Milligan, Mario Fabrizi and
Leo McKern.
(11 minutes)

The entire action takes place in a field. There is no plot or dialogue.

Sellers and Milligan appear with James Villiers in a cinema commercial for Benson
and Hedges cigarettes, made in 1974.

The Goons have on the whole done rather better separately than together in films.
Sellers, of course, has become an international star; notable films include *The
Ladykillers, The Smallest Show on Earth, I'm All Right, Jack, Two-Way Stretch,
Only Two Can Play, Lolita, The Pink Panther, Dr. Strangelove*, and *Mr. Topaze*
(which he also directed).
    Milligan has appeared in supporting roles in a number of films (notably as
Raquel Welch's husband in *The Three Musketeers*); he starred in a pleasant comedy
called *Postman's Knock* in 1962, also collaborating with Jack Trevor Story on the
screenplay. Other films include *Watch Your Stern, Suspect*, and *Invasion Quartet*.
    Secombe has appeared less frequently; principally *Davy, Oliver*, and *Song of
Norway*.

156

8: PUBLISHED GOON SHOW SCRIPTS

Series/number references are given; it should be noted that, although the titles are given reasonably accurately, a few shows have been incorrectly dated in the books. The titles are quoted here as they are given in the books. The scripts are as originally written; the broadcast versions contain slight deviations from the texts and occasional cuts.

THE GOON SHOW SCRIPTS—Woburn Press (hardback), Sphere Books (paperback)

5/3	The Dreaded Batter Pudding Hurler (of Bexhill-on-Sea)
5/4	The Phantom Head Shaver (of Brighton)
5/5	The Affair of the Lone Banana
5/6	The Canal
6/4	Napoleon's Piano
6/7	Foiled by President Fred
6/16	The Mighty Wurlitzer
6/15	The Hastings Flyer
6/20	The House of Teeth

MORE GOON SHOW SCRIPTS—Woburn Press (hardback), Sphere Books (paperback)
N.B. The 'Goonology' in this book is extremely inaccurate and misleading.

9/9	Battle of Spion Kop
9/10	Ned's Atomic Dustbin
9/11	The Spy, or Who is Pink Oboe
9/12	Call of the West
9/14	The Scarlet Capsule
9/15	The Tay Bridge Disaster
9/16	The Gold Plate Robbery
9/17	The £50 Cure

THE BOOK OF THE GOONS—Robson Books (hardback), Corgi Books (paperback)

6/12	The Terrible Revenge of Fred Fumanchu
8/16	The Great String Robberies
8/23	The Spon Plague
10/2	Tales of Men's Shirts
10/4	Robin's Post

This book also contains, by courtesy of Whacklow, Futtle & Crun (Commissioners for Oaths, Threats Issued), the authentic, unexpurgated inter-Goonal Correspondence of Certain Naughty Gentlemen and Sundry Others, alias Peter Sellers, Harry Secombe and Spike Milligan, including photographs by Snowdon and drawings by the Goons.

Readers may be interested to note the existence of The Goon Show Preservation Society, about which information may be obtained from Michael Coveney, 7 Frances Gardens, Ramsgate, Kent CT11 8AF.

INDEX

160